FAGE Total

ALL NATURAL GREEK YOGHURT

D1349431

Total

GREEK YOGHURT
COOKBOOK

Total

GREEK YOGHURT
COOKBOOK

OVER 120 FRESH AND HEALTHY IDEAS
FOR GREEK YOGHURT

SOPHIE MICHELL

PHOTOGRAPHY BY EMMA LEE
KYLE BOOKS

I dedicate this book to my Greek best friend Girgos, who died too young and too unexpectedly. Thank you for teaching me so much about Greek food. I still miss you.

First published in Great Britain in 2014 by Kyle Books,
an imprint of Kyle Cathie Ltd
192–198 Vauxhall Bridge Road, London SW1V 1DX

general.enquiries@kylebooks.com
www.kylebooks.com

10 9 8 7 6 5 4 3 2 1

ISBN 978 0 85783 263 4

Project Editor: Tara O'Sullivan
Copy Editor: Jane Bamforth
Concept and Introduction: Alison White (FAGE)
Designer: Miranda Harvey
Photographer: Emma Lee
Food Stylist: Annie Rigg
Prop Stylist: Joanna Harris
Production: Nic Jones and Gemma John

A Cataloguing in Publication record for this title is available from the British Library.

Colour reproduction by ALTA London
Printed and bound in China by C & C Offset Printing Co., Ltd

CONTENTS

WELCOME TO THE WONDERFUL WORLD OF TOTAL GREEK YOGHURT

For decades, if not centuries, Greek yoghurt has been an essential element of the Mediterranean diet. The reason for this is that Greek yoghurt is very special. Not only does it taste delicious, but Greek yoghurt – in particular TOTAL Greek Yoghurt – is incredibly versatile and an extraordinary source of nutrition.

Traditionally associated with breakfast, Greek yoghurt often conjures up fond memories of sun-drenched holidays and lazy al fresco mornings where there's no better way to start the day than with thick, creamy Greek yoghurt drizzled with Attica honey and topped with a sprinkling of nuts. These lovely holiday memories often remain, long after the holiday ends.

So it's not surprising that many visitors to Greece attempt to replicate their culinary memories once they are home. As a consequence, the popularity of Greek yoghurt has truly flourished, along with an understanding that this delicious, nutrient-rich yoghurt has great potential and is much more than just a tasty and healthy breakfast choice.

Over the years, foodies, cooks and chefs, (like our brilliant author Sophie Michell, who as well as appearing on TV and at various exciting pop ups is also Britain's youngest female executive chef), have been inspired by TOTAL Greek Yoghurt, using it not only in its purest form but also as an ingredient to add depth and flavour to a range of sweet and savoury recipes, from simple snacks such as Sweet Potato Fries with Avocado and Yoghurt Dip (page 16) to more complex dishes like Duck Kebabs with Rose Raita and Pilau Rice (page 106). It's not just the tangy flavour of TOTAL that foodies rave about – the benefits are also something to celebrate. Using Greek yoghurt as a natural alternative to cream, crème fraîche, mayonnaise or cream cheese can help reduce calorie and fat intake and help maintain a healthy lifestyle.

Ever since we first introduced TOTAL Greek Yoghurt to the UK in 1983, we have spent many hours experimenting in our kitchen, soaking up gastronomic inspiration and developing mouth-watering, lip-smackingly delicious recipes. We already share hundreds of recipes and ideas on our website (uk.fage.eu) but we thought it was time to compile a beautiful book of healthy, awe-inspiring recipes, influenced by Mediterranean cooking, with our own exciting twists.

And so we hooked up with Sophie to develop this book, made up of original recipes from Sophie and a selection of recipes from our archives given Sophie's unique treatment, which we hope will inspire and encourage you to get the very best from TOTAL yoghurt. We have no doubt that some of these recipes will become firm favourites with family and friends. We'd love to hear what you think. Share your views on any of our social network sites or email us at: customercareteam@totalgreekyoghurt.com

The Total Yoghurteers
#TryTotal

HOW IS IT MADE?

TOTAL Greek Yoghurt is naturally produced from cows' milk and our very own live active yoghurt cultures. This helps create its signature taste. Four litres of pasteurised cows' milk are used to make every litre of TOTAL Greek Yoghurt, which is then strained to remove all of the watery whey, leaving only the thick, velvety texture and unrivalled taste of our creamy yoghurt.

Made in the traditional Greek way, with all-natural ingredients and simple preparation, we believe TOTAL Greek Yoghurt to be unique. You won't find any added sugar, sweeteners, thickeners, powdered milk or preservatives in our yoghurt.

WHY IS TOTAL GREEK YOGHURT SPECIAL?

TOTAL Greek Yoghurt is the most popular yoghurt in Greece and also the best-selling brand of Greek yoghurt in the UK. In addition to its distinct, creamy taste and thick, luxurious texture, it has a great nutrient profile. It's a good source of calcium, contains less lactose and carbohydrates than regular yoghurt and, because it is strained, it boasts almost twice the protein of regular yoghurt, which is why it is especially popular with athletes and sporty types.

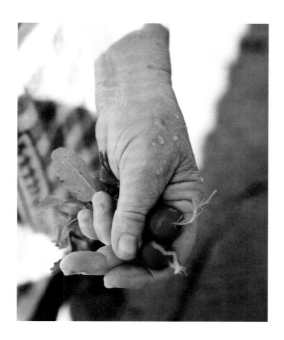

THE HISTORY OF TOTAL GREEK YOGHURT PRODUCTION

TOTAL Greek Yoghurt is made by FAGE (pronounced *fa-yeh*) who have created products loved by consumers around the globe.

Our story began in 1926 with the first dairy shop in Athens, Greece, which became known for its delicious, creamy, one-of-a-kind yoghurt. The shop was established by the family of Athanassios Filippou, the grandfather of FAGE's current Chief Executive Officer and Chairman of the Board. In 1954, under the guidance of his father and FAGE founder Athanassios, Ioannis Filippou helped to create the first wholesale distribution network for yoghurt in Greece. Ten years later, in 1964, Ioannis and his brother Kyriakos opened the company's first yoghurt production facility in Galatsi, a small suburb in Athens.

In 1975, when the FAGE yoghurt plant was relocated from Galatsi to another suburb of Athens, Metamorfosi, FAGE was the first company to introduce branded yoghurt products to the Greek market. No-one could have predicted the success which was to follow – the yoghurt market, first in Greece, and then internationally, was revolutionised in subsequent years.

From its roots as a local Athens dairy producer, FAGE expanded throughout Greece and then began exporting, first to the United Kingdom in 1983, and then to Italy and many other countries. Today, consumers enjoy FAGE's famous TOTAL Greek Yoghurt in over 40 different countries and the brand, and its reputation for quality, are trusted by millions of consumers worldwide.

THE CONCEPT OF OUR COOKERY BOOK

You've probably realised by now that we're particularly passionate about our yoghurt – both its virtues and its uses. So we set out to produce a cookbook that would demonstrate that healthier cooking needn't be boring. In fact by using a product like TOTAL and other fine ingredients, you can enjoy nutritious meals that are also exceptionally tasty.

It's important to remember that healthier eating is not about cutting the things you love out of your diet. It's about using them wisely and understanding where you can make intelligent swaps so that you don't feel you are missing out on any of life's culinary delights. Over the years we've loved hearing how TOTAL has added value to our customers' lifestyles. Not only can it add life to curries, soups and casseroles or act as a replacement for butter or oil in baking, it can also be used to create healthier versions of dishes that you may feel are a bit too indulgent for everyday consumption.

It's really easy to introduce Greek yoghurt into your cooking and, once you have been using it for a little while, we're certain you'll be inspired to try more recipes – from family meals like Smoked Cheddar, Gruyère and Mozzarella Macaroni Cheese (page 74) or dishes for entertaining such as Potato Rösti and Smoked Salmon with Vodka-Spiked Yoghurt and Keta (page 98) to cakes such as Red Velvet Cupcakes with Yoghurt Frosting (page 154) and treats like frozen yoghurt Lollies (page 178).

THE TOTAL SWAP COUNTER

As mentioned previously, TOTAL Greek Yoghurt is a healthier (and even more delicious) alternative to many other creamy ingredients. You can see from our Total-ly Intelligent Eating chart below that by swapping less healthy ingredients for TOTAL, you can make savings on fat content and calories. And another bonus is that you'll be adding extra protein to your diet. Protein helps us to feel fuller for longer and is important for growth and repair of the body and maintenance of general good health.

OTHER HEALTHY SWAPS TO TRY....

Try sweet potatoes or squash instead of white potatoes. Sweet potatoes have a much lower GI (Glycaemic Index) and are packed with nutrients.

Choose dark chocolate instead of milk chocolate.

Swap white pasta, bread and rice for wholemeal pasta and bread and brown rice – they contain fewer starchy carbohydrates.

Serve cauliflower 'rice' instead of white rice - whizz up raw cauliflower florets in a blender, then cook the 'rice' in a microwave on high for a couple of minutes.

Buy turkey mince instead of beef or pork mince.

Product	Calories (kCal) (per 100g)	Protein (per 100g)	Sugar (per 100g)	Fat content (per 100g)	Fat saturated (per 100g)
TOTAL 0% Greek Yoghurt	57	10.3	4	0	0
*Fat-free Greek-style yoghurt	60	6.1	8.7	0.1	0.1
TOTAL 2% Greek Yoghurt	73	9.9	3.8	2	1.3
TOTAL Greek Yoghurt, Classic	96	9	3.8	5	3.6
*Greek-style yoghurt	109	3.6	5	8.3	5.2
*Extra light cream cheese	111	4	6	5.2	4
*Half-fat sour cream	130	5.5	7.3	8.5	4.6
*Extra light salad cream	144	2	8.2	7.3	0.8
*Half-fat creme fraiche	166	2.9	3.5	14	10
*Single cream	188	2.6	3.9	18	11.2
*Original cream cheese	240	5.6	2.8	25.6	18
*Vanilla ice cream	270	5	21	18	11
*Condensed milk	325	8	56	8	5.2
*Salad cream	336	1.6	17.5	27	2
*Whipping cream	370	1.9	3	38.9	38.9
*Double cream	445	1.7	2.6	47.5	29.7
*Mayonnaise	722	1	2	79.1	6
*Butter	737	0.6	0.7	81.3	50.4

*Based on leading brand or supermarket own brand

A WORD FROM SOPHIE MICHELL

'My family have lived in Greece for 10 years and I have been going there since I was two with my mother. I have always loved the food of Greece. Apparently even when I was tiny I would sit in a Taverna eating olives and strong feta cheese happily, well into the balmy evenings. So Greece really feels like home to me.

'The purity of life on the island of Crete (where we have a house) is amazing – the old traditions and surrounding nature restore me when I visit.

'In particular I find the food there a tonic to my hectic lifestyle and rich diet in London. The quality of the ingredients is the most important factor in Greece, and simplicity comes in a close second – everything tastes so fresh and clean. It wakes up your body, along with the stark sunshine and azure sea.

'When I was approached by TOTAL Greek Yoghurt to write this book, I jumped at the chance. I cook with TOTAL Greek Yoghurt all the time in Greece and I love how versatile it is. I have also used it to replace higher fat products in my cooking and recipes for a long time, so the collaboration seemed perfect – plus I finally get to write some of my favourite Greek recipes down!

'For me, the best quality about TOTAL Greek Yoghurt is the fact that the recipe has barely changed since the 1920s. Provenance like that is what is so important and what makes my cooking come to life.

'So enjoy the book and bring a bit of the Greek sunshine to your everyday cooking with the help of TOTAL Greek Yoghurt!'

 You can spot Sophie's original recipes at a glance by looking out for this signature.

SMALL PLATES & SOUPS

SWEET POTATO FRIES WITH AVOCADO AND YOGHURT DIP

 Avocado is finally getting the recognition that it deserves. Its pale green creaminess and rich good fats are becoming more and more popular. It wasn't long ago that people used to avoid it due to it being higher in calories than most vegetables, and this ignorance used to really upset me. I have it almost every morning on rye toast, but made into a dip with the added protein of the yoghurt and served with low GI sweet potato chips, it is a winner.

SERVES 2 AS A SNACK

FOR THE FRIES
2 sweet potatoes, scrubbed and unpeeled
½ teaspoon garlic salt
½ teaspoon smoked paprika
200ml light olive oil
sea salt and freshly ground black pepper

FOR THE DIP
3 ripe avocados, halved and stoned
1 tablespoon freshly chopped coriander, plus
    extra to garnish
200g 2% Greek yoghurt
1 teaspoon lime juice

Preheat the oven to 200°C/gas mark 6.

Using a sharp knife, slice the sweet potatoes lengthways into chip-like batons.

Place the garlic salt, paprika, olive oil and seasoning in a large bowl and toss the sweet potato chips in it to coat thoroughly. Transfer the chips to a non-stick baking tray and cook for 40 minutes.

Whilst the chips are cooking, make the dip. Scoop the avocado flesh into a medium-sized bowl and mash with a fork. Stir in the coriander, yoghurt and lime juice, season to taste and serve, with an extra scattering of coriander and the sweet potato fries.

IF THE DIP IS READY AND YOUR CHIPS ARE STILL COOKING, PLACE THE AVOCADO STONE IN THE BOWL WITH THE DIP AND COVER WITH CLINGFILM – THIS WILL STOP THE DIP FROM TURNING BROWN

POTATO AND THYME GRATIN

 Who isn't into creamy, layered, garlicky potatoes? It's a classic combo, but can sometimes be quite rich. The Greek yoghurt works well here, lightening the dish in flavour and fat content.

SERVES 4

750g medium-sized floury potatoes, such as
    Maris Piper, unpeeled and scrubbed
100g butter
2 garlic cloves, crushed
bunch of thyme sprigs, leaves removed
170g Classic Greek yoghurt
100g Gruyère, grated
salt and freshly ground black pepper

Preheat the oven to 180°C/gas mark 4.

Place the potatoes in a saucepan of salted water and bring to the boil, then simmer for 20 minutes until tender. Drain and set aside to cool. Peel the skins off the cooled potatoes and cut them into 5mm slices. Place the potato slices in a large bowl.

Melt the butter in a small pan, add the crushed garlic and thyme leaves and heat through for about 1 minute. Pour the butter mixture and yoghurt over the potatoes, season well and carefully turn the potato slices to coat.

Arrange the potato slices in a 15–20cm baking dish. Sprinkle the Gruyère over and bake for 20 minutes.

BY USING TOTAL GREEK YOGHURT IN THIS DISH INSTEAD OF DOUBLE CREAM, YOU'VE JUST REDUCED THE FAT CONTENT BY 90%

BUTTERNUT SQUASH AND SAGE BAKE

 Butternut squash is such a versatile ingredient, I struggle not to overuse it in my menus. Sage is its perfect mate and, combined with the Parmesan and creamy yoghurt,this bake is a blinder. This goes with so many dishes – roast leg of lamb would be my fave, though.

SERVES 4

1 butternut squash (approximately 800g), peeled, deseeded and chopped into 4cm cubes
1 teaspoon olive oil
small bunch of fresh sage leaves, roughly torn
300g Classic Greek yoghurt
200g Parmesan, grated
salt and freshly ground black pepper

Preheat the oven to 180°C/gas mark 4.

Place the squash cubes in a shallow ovenproof serving dish, approximately 15 x 20cm. Season well, drizzle the oil over and toss to coat. Roast for 30 minutes. Remove the dish from the oven and mix in the torn sage leaves and yoghurt. Sprinkle the cheese over and cook for a further 20–30 minutes, or until the squash is tender.

POLENTA AND PARMESAN CHIPS
WITH YOGHURT AND TRUFFLE DIP

 I'm afraid to say I'm a bit truffle mad and, yes, I would like to have fresh white truffles grated on EVERYTHING I EAT. Unfortunately, I am not a billionaire and they have a short season, but I do use a bit of good-quality white truffle oil now and again. These are indulgent, sexy chips with a decadent-tasting dip, and the yoghurt gives it a tangy freshness that is needed. These chips also go with lots of other dishes; I love to serve them with a caviar and yoghurt dip, but, again, more in my imaginary billionaire life than in reality.

SERVES 4 AS A SNACK

FOR THE CHIPS
1 litre hot vegetable stock
50g butter
200g quick-cook polenta
100g Parmesan, grated
100ml sunflower or vegetable oil
sea salt and freshly ground black pepper

FOR THE DIP
1 teaspoon truffle oil
1 tablespoon chopped canned truffle or truffle paste
1 tablespoon snipped chives
200g Classic Greek yoghurt

Line an 18 x 25cm baking tray with greaseproof paper.

Place the stock and butter in a large saucepan and bring to the boil. Quickly pour in the polenta and stir well to remove any lumps. Reduce the heat to low and simmer for 15 minutes, stirring continuously until all the liquid has been absorbed and the mixture has thickened. Add the Parmesan, stir again for 30 seconds and season with salt and pepper.

Spoon the polenta mixture into the lined tray and leave to cool to room temperature, then transfer to the fridge for 20 minutes to set.

To make the dip, place the truffle oil, chopped truffle or paste, chives and yoghurt in a small bowl. Stir to mix well and season to taste.

With a palette knife or spatula, cut the set polenta into approximately 20 chunky chips. Heat the sunflower or vegetable oil in a large non-stick frying pan over a medium-high heat and, when hot, fry the chips in batches for about 5 minutes, until golden and crispy on all sides. Remove from the oil using a slotted spoon and drain on kitchen paper. Transfer to a tray in a warm oven whilst you cook the remaining batches.

Serve the polenta chips hot with the dip.

DIPS LIKE THIS ARE OFTEN MADE WITH MAYONNAISE — BY USING TOTAL GREEK YOGHURT INSTEAD, YOU REDUCE THE CALORIES BY 87%

DOLMADES

 My family live in Crete, Greece, which in my mind
has some of the best food in the country. This is my
favourite recipe for dolmades – the addition of meat
is unusual, but it adds much more flavour. You must
always serve dolmades with cool Greek yoghurt
on the side. At home in Crete I use the young vine
leaves from our two hundred-year-old grapevine,
which is wonderful, but you can easily find them
in supermarkets now. I also use stuffed courgette
flowers when in season, but they are much more
delicate and if I use them, I omit the lamb.

MAKES 16–20 DOLMADES

100g basmati rice
200g jar of vine leaves in brine, drained
100ml extra-virgin olive oil
200g minced lamb
2 garlic cloves, crushed
1 onion, finely chopped
50g sultanas
50g pine nuts
1 teaspoon ground cinnamon
1 teaspoon dried oregano
1 tablespoon tomato purée
small handful of freshly chopped flat-leaf parsley
juice of 1 lemon
salt and freshly ground black pepper
Classic Greek yoghurt, to serve

Cook the rice according to the packet instructions.
Drain if necessary and set aside.

Soak the drained vine leaves in boiling water for
5 minutes, then drain and set aside to cool.

Place a large frying pan over a medium heat and
pour in half the olive oil, add the lamb, garlic and
onion and fry for about 10 minutes until the mixture
starts to turn golden.

Add the sultanas, pine nuts, cinnamon and oregano
and fry for a further 5 minutes. Finally add 50ml
cold water and the tomato purée, stir well and cook
for 5 minutes. Stir in the cooked rice and the parsley,
season well and set aside to cool.

Preheat the oven to 160°C/gas mark 3.

Place 1 vine leaf on a chopping board, with the veins
facing up, and spoon 1 dessertspoon of filling onto
the centre of the leaf. Carefully fold in the sides of
the leaf and then tightly roll it up – the trick is not
to add too much filling. Place the stuffed leaf into a
15x20cm ovenproof dish. Repeat using the remaining
filling, packing the stuffed leaves tightly together in
the dish.

Mix the remaining oil with 50ml hot water and the
lemon juice. Pour over the vine leaves, season, cover
with foil and bake for 1 hour.

Serve the dolamades warm with a big dollop of
yoghurt on the side. They are also great served
chilled, as a snack or starter.

BARBECUED WATERMELON WITH AGAVE AND GREEK YOGHURT

This is a slightly different way to serve a fruit salad. Barbecuing the watermelon is fun and the charred flavour works well with the Greek yoghurt. Then the agave syrup adds sweetness, the chilli a bit of bite and the mint really lifts it. This recipe is inspired by one I wrote for a pre-work out snack for *Women's Health* magazine.

SERVES 4–6

1 watermelon, cut into slices
1 tablespoon olive oil
4 tablespoons agave syrup
pinch of chilli powder
small handful of chopped mint
0% Greek yoghurt, to serve

Preheat a barbecue (if using) or a griddle pan.

Rub the watermelon slices with the olive oil and cook on the barbecue or in the griddle pan for approximately 5 minutes on each side until lightly charred.

Drizzle the charred melon with the agave syrup and sprinkle with the chilli powder and mint. Serve with Greek yoghurt.

THERE IS MORE THAN 10G OF PROTEIN IN 100G TOTAL 0% GREEK YOGHURT

BEETROOT SALAD WITH YOGHURT, DILL AND WALNUT DRESSING

 Vegetables taste amazing in Greece as they're almost always fresh, locally grown and in season. I particularly love the beetroot grown in Greece. It's a world away from the vacuum-packed vinegary offerings found in supermarkets and it's so easy to boil or roast and enjoy in a simple salad like this one. The Greek yoghurt, walnut and dill dressing is also Greece-inspired, and I love to serve this dish as an accompaniment to lamb chops or grilled fish.

SERVES 4

800g medium-sized raw beetroots, unpeeled
50ml olive oil
sea salt and freshly ground black pepper

FOR THE DRESSING

150g walnuts
340g Classic Greek yoghurt
2 garlic cloves, finely chopped
juice of 1 lemon
handful of chopped dill

Preheat the oven to 180°C/gas mark 4.

Rub the beetroot all over with the olive oil and season well. Place on a baking tray, cover with foil and roast for 45–60 minutes or until a skewer can be easily inserted into the centre.

Take the beetroot out of the oven and set aside to cool completely. When cool enough to handle, rub the skin off with your fingers (preferably wearing gloves to avoid staining your skin).

Meanwhile, make the dressing. Finely chop most of the walnuts, reserving a few for garnish. Mix together the yoghurt, garlic, chopped walnuts, lemon juice and dill in a small bowl and season to taste.

Cut the beetroot into wedges and serve on a platter or in a bowl, with big dollops of the yoghurt dressing. Roughly crush the remaining walnuts and sprinkle over to garnish.

MINTED PEA AND BEAN SALAD
WITH SALTED GREEK YOGHURT

Peas are often served as an afterthought, overboiled and browning on the side of a plate of meat. I love them in summer salads like this one, bright green and gorgeous. You will notice that I have strained the yoghurt further and made it almost into a cheese; don't be put off by this, it's quite satisfying seeing a new product emerge. The process takes 24 hours, so begin the day before.

SERVES 4

FOR THE SALAD
500g Classic Greek yoghurt
150g frozen peas
150g frozen broad beans
150g wild rocket
2 Little Gem lettuces, leaves torn
bunch of spring onions, chopped
salt and freshly ground black pepper
mint leaves, to garnish

FOR THE DRESSING
50g Classic Greek yoghurt
1 teaspoon wholegrain mustard
1 tablespoon runny honey
2 tablespoons olive oil
1 tablespoon white wine vinegar

To make the salted Greek yoghurt, season the 500g of yoghurt with salt and pepper, place it in a clean tea towel or muslin cloth and tie the material tightly. Suspend the wrapped yoghurt over a bowl and place in the fridge for 24 hours – the yoghurt will separate and any liquid will drip into the bowl.

On the day of making, defrost the peas and beans, then unshell the broad beans.

Combine all the dressing ingredients in a small jug and stir well.

In a serving bowl, toss the wild rocket, lettuce leaves, peas, beans and spring onions together. Remove the strained yoghurt from the material and crumble it over the top of the salad.

Pour over the dressing and garnish with fresh mint just before serving.

THE DRESSING WILL KEEP, COVERED, FOR UP TO 3 DAYS IN THE FRIDGE

AUBERGINE AND FENNEL FRITTERS WITH FENNEL YOGHURT

This recipe comes from the Total Greek Yoghurt archives. I changed it slightly, but I love the way the crisp fritters contrast with the cooling fennel yoghurt dip on the side. I also love layering up flavours – having the cooked fennel as well as fennel seeds in the dip is a great example.

SERVES 4 AS A STARTER

1 teaspoon fennel seeds
85g 2% Greek yoghurt
200ml milk (any type)
1 aubergine, cut into 1cm rounds
1 fennel bulb, thickly sliced
100g plain white flour
vegetable or sunflower oil, for frying
salt and freshly ground black pepper

Mix the fennel seeds and yoghurt together in a bowl and chill.

Pour the milk into a shallow dish, add the aubergine and fennel slices and press down to cover them completely with the milk.

Put the flour in another shallow dish and season. Take the aubergine and fennel slices from the milk and dust with the flour. Repeat this with the milk and flour to give a second coating.

Pour about 4cm of oil into a large heavy-based pan. Heat the oil to 180°C (measure the temperature using a thermometer, or drop a small piece of white bread into the oil – if it fizzes and turns golden brown, the oil is hot enough).

Cook the aubergine and fennel slices until crisp and golden for 5–6 minutes, in batches if necessary. Turn them as they cook to get both sides golden. Remove from the oil using a slotted spoon and drain on kitchen paper. Serve the fritters with the yoghurt dip.

CRISPY FALAFEL WITH TOASTED CUMIN SEEDS AND GARLIC YOGHURT

Falafels are a staple dish in the Middle East and when I lived in Beirut I really started to appreciate how tasty and what a great healthy bite they are. Crisp hot patties, wrapped up with fresh herbs, pickles, and the all important yoghurt sauce – you can't beat it! This recipe was from the Total Yoghurt archives and it takes me straight back to Beirut.

SERVES 4–6

FOR THE FALAFEL
400g dry chickpeas, soaked in cold water for 6 hours
40g fresh coriander, chopped
75g fresh ginger, chopped
4 chillies
2 garlic cloves
7 spring onions
salt and freshly ground black pepper
vegetable oil, for frying

FOR THE DRESSING
340g 2% Greek yoghurt
1 teaspoon toasted cumin seeds
1 garlic clove, finely chopped

TO SERVE
4–6 flatbreads
200g pickled gherkins, sliced
small handful of mint leaves, torn

To make the falafel, drain the chickpeas and bung them, along with all the other falafel ingredients except the vegetable oil, into a food processor. Whizz up until they resemble breadcrumbs in texture. To mould into shape, take a large dessertspoon full of mixture and press the spoon into the palm of your hand. This will mould the mixture into an egg-like shape.

To cook the falafel, heat 8cm of vegetable oil in a pan to about 180°C (measure the temperature using a thermometer, or drop a small piece of white bread into the oil – if it fizzes and turns golden brown, the oil is hot enough). Fry the falafel until golden, in batches if necessary. Drain on kitchen paper before serving.

To make the dressing, mix all the dressing ingredients together in a bowl and then season.

To serve, heat up the flatbreads, and spread with some of the yoghurt. Pile on the falafels, gherkins and mint leaves. Roll up and eat!

SPICED COURGETTES WITH SRIRACHA CHILLI DIP

This is a recipe from the Total Greek Yoghurt archive. I brought it up to date with the addition of Sriracha chilli sauce, which is very popular in the US and available in most supermarkets in the UK. It really packs a punch and has a great flavour.

SERVES 4

FOR THE DIP
250g 2% Greek yoghurt
2 tablespoons Sriracha chilli sauce or a hot spicy
    sauce alternative

FOR THE COURGETTES
200g plain white flour
1 teaspoon smoked paprika
1 teaspoon garlic granules
200ml milk (any type)
2 large courgettes, cut into 6cm-long batons
vegetable oil, for frying

Line a baking tray with baking parchment.

Mix the yoghurt and chilli sauce together in a small bowl and set aside.

In a shallow bowl, mix the flour, paprika and garlic granules together. Pour the milk into a separate shallow bowl.

Dip each courgette baton into the milk and then coat in the flour and spice mix. Make sure each baton is completely coated in the flour mixture. Place the batons on the lined tray.

Pour about 5cm of oil into a large heavy-based pan. Heat the oil to 180°C (measure the temperature using a thermometer, or drop a small piece of white bread into the oil – if it fizzes and turns golden brown, the oil is hot enough).

Cook the batons in batches. When each batch has been frying for a few seconds, gently stir the oil to make sure the batons do not stick together. When the batons turn golden brown, remove them using a slotted spoon and drain on kitchen paper. Keep the batons hot by placing them on a tray in a warm oven whilst you cook the remaining batches.

Serve the batons hot with the chilli dip.

TARAMASALATA WITH GREEN OLIVE AND LEMON BREAD

Homemade taramasalata is so vastly superior to shop-bought versions that it really is worth making your own. Also, it comes out a lovely pale pink creamy colour, as opposed to lurid pink. Serve this with some ice-cold ouzo for a real Greek meze feel.

SERVES 2

FOR THE TARAMASALATA
100g Classic Greek yoghurt
2 x 100g cans soft cod roes
75g white bread, crusts removed, or 50g crustless bread
1 garlic clove, crushed
2 tablespoons lemon juice
good pinch of cayenne pepper, plus extra to garnish
fresh flat-leaf parsley, to garnish

FOR THE BREAD
100g Classic Greek yoghurt
1 tablespoon runny honey
7g sachet fast-action dried yeast
250g strong white bread flour, plus extra for dusting
75g pitted green olives, roughly chopped
zest of 1 lemon
1 teaspoon olive oil
sprig of fresh rosemary

For the taramasalata, put all the ingredients, except the parsley, in a food processor and blitz until smooth. Spoon into a serving dish and sprinkle with a little extra cayenne. Cover and chill for at least 1 hour.

To make the bread, mix the yoghurt, honey and yeast with 5 tablespoons boiling water. Put the flour in a large bowl, add the yoghurt mixture and stir well. Bring the dough together with your hands, then turn out onto a lightly floured surface. Squeeze out any excess brine from the olives and then knead into the dough for 2 minutes, along with the lemon zest.

Line a large baking sheet with baking parchment. Divide the dough into two halves and roll into balls. Place on the baking sheet and flatten each ball into a disc about 15cm in diameter. Cover with lightly oiled clingfilm and leave to rise for 30 minutes.

Preheat the oven to 200°C/gas mark 6. Remove the clingfilm from the dough, then dimple the surface thoroughly with your fingertips. Bake for 15 minutes until golden. Check the underside of the bread is cooked too – if not, bake for a further 2–3 minutes.

Cool slightly, then brush with the oil and rub with the rosemary. Cut into triangles.

Garnish the taramasalata with the parsley and serve with the bread triangles.

SMOKED TROUT PÂTÉ WITH BUCKWHEAT BLINIS

Smoked trout pâté is super-quick to make and is lovely as a nibble. The Greek yoghurt lightens the flavour, but adds fewer calories than the traditionally used crème fraîche or cream cheese. The buckwheat blinis are also great and quick to make. I use them all the time, and they are good with smoked salmon and caviar, too.

MAKES APPROXIMATELY 40 TOPPED BLINIS

FOR THE BLINIS
150g 2% Greek yoghurt
150g plain buckwheat flour
1 medium egg
1 teaspoon bicarbonate of soda
spray oil

FOR THE PÂTÉ
225g hot-smoked trout or hot-smoked salmon
3 tablespoons baby capers in brine, drained
zest of 1 lemon
2 tablespoons lemon juice
½ small bunch dill, finely chopped, plus extra to garnish
125g 2% Greek yoghurt
freshly ground black pepper
lemon slices, quartered, to garnish

In a large bowl, mix together all the blini ingredients, except the spray oil. Add 150ml cold water and stir well until the batter is smooth. Set aside for 5 minutes.

Heat a large non-stick frying pan over a low-medium heat and spray with oil. Add 8 teaspoonfuls of batter to the pan, spacing each at least 3cm apart. Cook for 1–1½ minutes until bubbles appear on the surface. Turn over using a spatula or fish slice and cook for 1 minute. Transfer to a plate.

Wipe the pan with kitchen paper, spray with oil, and repeat until all the batter has been used.

To make the pâté, put the trout or salmon, capers and lemon zest in a food processor and pulse until coarse. Add the lemon juice, dill, yoghurt and lots of black pepper and pulse again to combine.

Spoon small spoonfuls of the pâté onto each blini, garnish with dill and lemon slices and serve.

TOTAL +1

Total Greek Yoghurt is versatile and delicious, and as well as being a great ingredient to use in a variety of dishes, it can also take centre stage in simple recipes like these ones, where just one ingredient is added to Total Greek Yoghurt to create a wealth of sweet and savoury options. Why not come up with your own Total +1 ideas?

LABNEH

SERVES 4

1 teaspoon sea salt
340g Classic Greek yoghurt
za'atar and olive oil, to serve

Mix the salt and yoghurt together in a small bowl. Rinse a piece of muslin or a clean tea towel under cold running water and then spread it out over a medium bowl. Spoon the yoghurt mixture in the centre of the cloth, gather the edges up around the outside and tie up the material tightly with string. Suspend the wrapped yoghurt over the bowl and leave in the fridge for 24 hours. This separates the whey and leaves you with a lovely tangy cream cheese. I like to serve it with za'atar and olive oil.

ALMOND BUTTER SPREAD

SERVES 4

170g 2% Greek yoghurt
2 tablespoons almond butter

Mix the yoghurt and almond butter together in a small bowl until well combined. Spread on all sorts of lovely stuff, like toasted crumpets or pancakes, use it as frosting for cupcakes, or even dip slices of apple into it for a healthy snack.

YOGHURT-DIPPED STRAWBERRIES

SERVES 4

170g Classic Greek yoghurt
15 strawberries

Line a baking tray with baking parchment.

Beat the yoghurt in a small bowl until smooth. Partially dip each strawberry into the yoghurt and place on the baking tray. Freeze for 1–3 hours and serve straight from the freezer as a snack.

CREAMY CHOCOLATE DIP

SERVES 4

75g good-quality dark chocolate, minimum 70 per cent cocoa solids, broken into small pieces
170g Classic Greek yoghurt

Place the chocolate in a small heatproof bowl over a pan of barely simmering water, stirring occasionally until melted. Remove from the heat, then stir in the yoghurt. This is a great dip for fruit.

MISO DIP

SERVES 4

2 tablespoons miso paste
170g 2% Greek yoghurt

Mix the miso and yoghurt together in a small bowl. Serve with grilled prawns or pork, or crudités.

BARBECUE DIP

SERVES 4

170g 0% Greek yoghurt
100ml good-quality barbecue sauce

Mix the yoghurt and barbecue sauce together in a small bowl. Serve with chicken wings, celery sticks and potato wedges.

CARAMELISED ONION DIP

SERVES 4

170g Classic Greek yoghurt
2 tablespoons caramelised onion marmalade

Mix the yoghurt and onion marmalade together in a small bowl. Serve with crisps or chips. Also good with grilled meats and in steak sandwiches and burgers.

CRAB CAKES WITH TARRAGON, CHIVE AND LEMON SAUCE

 Crab cakes are super popular and always one of our best-sellers at my restaurant, Pont St. We have unpasteurised, freshly picked white crab from Dorset delivered daily, but you can also buy whole crabs and pick out the meat – it's a long process, but quite fun. Failing that, find a good fishmonger and get them to do the hard work for you.

SERVES 4

400g white crab meat
150g brown crab meat
4 spring onions, finely chopped
1 tablespoon 0% Greek yoghurt
1 tablespoon chopped tarragon
1 tablespoon chopped chives
zest of 1 lemon
50g panko breadcrumbs
50ml olive oil, for frying
salad leaves, to serve
sea salt and freshly ground black pepper

FOR THE SAUCE

100g 0% Greek yoghurt
1 tablespoon chopped capers in brine, drained
    and rinsed
1 tablespoon chopped gherkins
1 tablespoon freshly chopped flat-leaf parsley
juice of 1 lemon
pinch of cayenne pepper

Line a baking tray with baking parchment.

Place the crab meats in a large mixing bowl and check thoroughly to make sure there are no pieces of shell.

Add the spring onions, yoghurt, herbs, lemon zest and breadcrumbs. Season and stir to thoroughly combine. Using your hands, shape the mixture into 12 even-sized patties. Transfer the patties to the lined tray and chill in the fridge for at least 30 minutes.

To make the sauce, place all the ingredients in a small jug, season and stir well, then set aside.

To cook the crab cakes, pour a splash of the oil into a large non-stick frying pan over a medium heat and fry the cakes for about 5 minutes on each side, until golden brown. If working in batches, keep the cooked crab cakes hot by placing them on a preheated baking tray in a warm oven whilst the remainder are cooking.

Serve the crab cakes with the sauce and some salad leaves.

KING PRAWN AND GINGER WONTONS WITH SWEET CHILLI AND CORIANDER DIPPING SAUCE

The original version of this recipe was written by Paul Merrett for Total Greek Yoghurt a while back. Like all of Paul's recipes, it really caught my eye. Paul was my first Head Chef in London and he really is talented. The yoghurt binds the filling in these wontons and adds a lovely creaminess.

MAKES 16 WONTONS

FOR THE DIPPING SAUCE
100g Classic Greek yoghurt
1 tablespoon sweet chilli sauce
1 tablespoon soy sauce
1 tablespoon freshly chopped coriander

FOR THE WONTONS
8 raw, peeled king prawns, 6 finely chopped and
    2 coarsely chopped
1 small egg, beaten
2 tablespoons double cream
1 tablespoon Classic Greek yoghurt
20g fresh ginger, peeled and finely grated
2 spring onions, finely diced
16 wonton wrappers
500ml vegetable oil
salt and freshly ground black pepper

To make the dipping sauce, combine all the ingredients together in a small bowl and set aside.

For the wonton filling, place the finely chopped prawns in a medium bowl with half the beaten egg and stir to combine thoroughly. Pour in the cream and yoghurt and mix together.

Stir in the coarsley chopped prawns, along with the ginger and spring onions, and season.

Take your first wonton wrapper, lay it flat on the work surface and put a teaspoonful of the filling mixture in the centre. Brush a little of the remaining beaten egg around the edges of the wonton wrapper and then lift up the edges and scrunch them together to make a little pouch (see picture). Repeat, using the remaining filling and wrappers, to make 16 wontons in total.

The wontons can be cooked immediately or kept in the fridge for up to 1 hour before cooking.

Heat the oil in a large, deep, heavy-based pan to 180°C (you can measure the temperature using a thermometer, or drop a small piece of white bread into the oil – once it fizzes and turns golden brown, the oil is hot enough).

Carefully place the wontons in the oil and fry, in batches if necessary, for 3 minutes until crispy and hot. Remove using a slotted spoon. If frying in batches, keep the cooked wontons warm on a warm plate covered with foil or a clean tea towel whilst you fry the remainder.

Drain the wontons on kitchen paper and serve immediately with the dipping sauce.

KING PRAWN COCKTAIL WITH
JALAPEÑOS, CORIANDER AND AVOCADO

 Ceviche is the Latin American way of cooking fish in a deliciously fresh citrus dressing and it's very fashionable right now. This prawn cocktail is ceviche-inspired – gorgeous king prawns in a lime and chilli marinade, topped with a creamy dollop of jalapeño-spiked yoghurt – fresh and perfect for summer.

SERVES 4

50ml tomato juice
juice of 2 limes
few dashes of Green Jalapeño Tabasco sauce
400g king prawns
150g cherry tomatoes, quartered
1 tablespoon finely chopped red onion
½ avocado, finely chopped
1 tablespoon torn coriander leaves
sea salt and freshly ground black pepper

TO SERVE

1 tablespoon diced jalapeños (from a jar)
170g Classic Greek yoghurt

In a large bowl, mix the tomato juice, lime juice and Tabasco sauce together, season to taste, then add the prawns, cherry tomatoes, red onion, avocado and coriander and stir to combine.

In a separate bowl, stir together the diced jalapeños and yoghurt and season. To serve, divide the prawn mixture between 4 glass dishes and top each with a big spoonful of spicy yoghurt.

BY USING TOTAL GREEK YOGHURT IN THIS DISH INSTEAD OF THE MAYONNAISE MORE COMMONLY USED FOR PRAWN COCKTAILS, YOU'VE JUST CUT OUT APPROXIMATELY 125G OF FAT

OYSTERS ROMANOFF

 So back to my imaginary billionaire lifestyle – these oysters, served with some bubbles pre-dinner, really make you feel special. I feel there is a sense of occasion with oysters, and I used to be quite purist about them, only eating them plain with lemon juice. However, they really are wonderful topped with Greek yoghurt and caviar – and I reckon they've got to be an aphrodisiac, too.

SERVES 2

12 oysters
2 lemons, cut into wedges
3 spring onions, finely chopped
200g Classic Greek yoghurt
150g caviar (see tip, right)
crushed ice, to serve

Wrap a tea towel over one hand to protect it and shuck the oysters carefully using an oyster knife. Try to keep the meat intact and the juice inside.

Squeeze a little lemon juice over each oyster, add a sprinkling of spring onions and a spoonful of yoghurt and top with the caviar. Serve immediately, preferably on a bed of ice.

LUMPFISH CAVIAR OR SALMON KETA ARE GREAT ALTERNATIVES TO PRICY STURGEON CAVIAR

MARINATED HERRINGS WITH PERNOD YOGHURT DRESSING

Marinated herrings are fantastic on rye bread toast. I often have them for breakfast or for a light lunch. They are traditionally served with sour cream, but the Greek yoghurt works really well here. The Pernod adds an aniseed touch and sweet acidity, too.

SERVES 2

85g Classic Greek yoghurt
25ml Pernod
2 tablespoons snipped chives, plus extra to garnish
2 large rollmop herrings
150g mixed salad leaves
2 cooked beetroots, cut into strips
4 slices of rye bread

Mix the yoghurt, Pernod and chives together in a small bowl. Roughly chop the rollmops into bite-sized pieces and mix with the yoghurt.

Place the salad leaves in a serving bowl, top with the herrings and beetroot strips and garnish with the extra chives. Toast the rye bread and serve with the salad.

CHORIZO AND TOASTED CORN FRITTERS WITH RED PEPPER SAUCE

These little fritters are packed full of flavour. One from the Total Greek Yoghurt archives again, and great for a child-friendly snack. They are quick and easy to make and feel really bright and summery. They are also easy to convert into a vegetarian option – I would use some feta instead of chorizo.

SERVES 4 AS A MAIN MEAL OR 6 AS A STARTER

2 corn on the cob
100g chorizo, diced
bunch of spring onions, sliced
1 garlic clove, crushed
100g self-raising flour
2 medium eggs
200g 2% Greek yoghurt
spray oil

FOR THE SAUCE

75g peeled roasted peppers in brine, drained and
    blotted on kitchen paper
zest and juice of 1 lime

Preheat the grill to high. Place the corn cobs on a grill rack and cook for 5–6 minutes, turning frequently, until the kernels turn deep golden. Set aside to cool slightly, then, using a sharp knife, slice off the kernels: stand each cob on its end and slice down for ease.

Meanwhile, heat a medium non-stick frying pan and add the chorizo. Cook over a medium heat for 5 minutes until some fat melts from the chorizo. Add the spring onions and garlic and cook for 2–3 minutes until soft.

In a bowl, mix together the flour, eggs, 125g of the yoghurt and 2 tablespoons of cold water. Add the corn and cooked chorizo mixture.

Spray a large non-stick frying pan with oil and add 4 tablespoonfuls of the batter, spacing each at least 3cm apart. Cook over a medium heat for 1–2 minutes until bubbles form on the surface. Turn and cook for 1 minute or until golden. Transfer to a warm plate. Repeat until all the batter has been used – this recipe makes 8–10 fritters.

For the sauce, whizz the peppers with the lime zest and juice in a food-processor until smooth. Mix in the remaining 75g yoghurt and serve with the fritters.

JALAPEÑO AND CHEESE CORNBREAD

Cornbread is one of those breads that is easy to make, but incredibly satisfying. This buttery, soft, slightly sweet bread is gorgeous served warm and great to make as a quick replacement for normal bread. Here it is speckled with chopped jalapeños for a little kick. I would serve this with some Mexican mole or the Chipotle Turkey and Black Turtle Bean Chilli on page 120.

MAKES 16 SQUARES

butter, for greasing
175g fine or instant polenta
125g plain white flour
1 tablespoon baking powder
2 tablespoons caster sugar
2 medium eggs, beaten
250g 0% Greek yoghurt
200ml skimmed milk
50g green jalapeños in brine (drained weight), chopped
125g feta, crumbled
salt and freshly ground black pepper

Preheat the oven to 180°C/gas mark 4. Grease a 20cm square cake tin and line it with baking parchment.

In a large bowl, mix together the polenta, flour, baking powder and sugar.

In a large jug, whisk together the eggs, yoghurt and milk and pour into the dry ingredients. Season and mix well until smooth.

Add roughly two-thirds of the chopped jalapeños and two-thirds of the crumbled cheese, stir to combine, then pour into the cake tin.

Scatter over the remaining jalapeños and cheese. Bake for 50 minutes to 1 hour until springy to the touch. If the bread browns too quickly during cooking, cover it loosely with foil.

Allow the bread to cool in the tin for 15 minutes, then cut it into 16 equal-sized squares and serve warm.

THAI CHICKEN CUPS

I travelled around South-east Asia a lot in my early teens with family and later by myself. The trips really inspired me and I still love cooking with the bold flavours from that part of the world, like the ones in this archive recipe. I like using lettuce for cups of salad and the yoghurt works surprisingly well with the Thai flavours. Very moreish!

SERVES 2

2 x 100g skinless chicken breast fillets
300ml hot chicken stock
zest and juice of 1 lime
2 teaspoons Thai red curry paste
½ teaspoon soft light brown sugar
handful of coriander leaves, roughly chopped, plus extra to garnish
125g 0% Greek yoghurt
1 medium carrot, cut into shreds or grated
1 small red pepper, finely sliced
8 Little Gem lettuce leaves
1 small red onion, cut into rings
25g unsalted peanuts, dry-fried and crushed

Put the chicken fillets in a small pan and add the stock. Pour over enough hot water to completely cover the chicken. Gently bring to the boil, reduce the heat and simmer for 20 minutes. Remove the chicken from the stock and set aside to cool. You can reserve the stock and use it in a soup or a risotto, if you like.

In a small frying pan, heat the lime zest and juice, curry paste and sugar until bubbling. Reduce the heat and cook until the liquid has evaporated, then set aside to cool.

In a medium bowl combine the coriander, yoghurt and lime mixture. Shred the cooled chicken, then add to the bowl and stir well.

Store the chicken and prepared vegetables in the fridge until ready to serve.

To assemble the cups, spoon the chicken, carrot and pepper into the lettuce leaves and garnish with the onion rings and crushed peanuts.

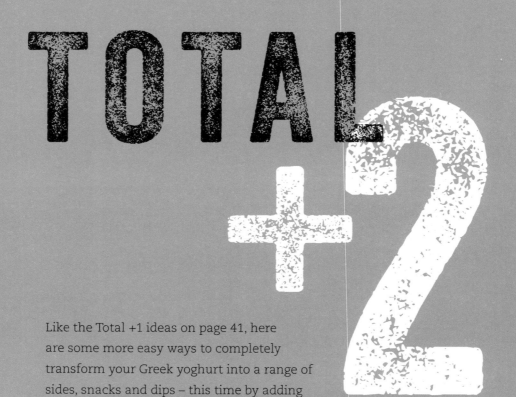

TOTAL +2

Like the Total +1 ideas on page 41, here are some more easy ways to completely transform your Greek yoghurt into a range of sides, snacks and dips – this time by adding just two ingredients. For some sweet +2 ideas, see page 151.

CREAMED NUTMEG SPINACH

SERVES 2

300g spinach
1 whole nutmeg, for grating
2 tablespoons Classic Greek yoghurt
salt and freshly ground pepper

Place a medium saucepan over a medium heat. Add the spinach and a splash of water, cover and steam for 5 minutes. Drain well and squeeze out any excess liquid and then return to the pan, off the heat. Season well and grate in a generous sprinkling of nutmeg, stir well, then add the yoghurt. Stir again and serve as a side dish.

PEA AND MINT CRUSH

SERVES 2

300g frozen peas, defrosted
1 tablespoon chopped mint
170g Classic Greek yoghurt
salt and freshly ground black pepper

Place the peas in a small pan with a splash of water and heat through over a medium heat. Add the mint and season well, then take off the heat. Using a hand-held electric blender, blitz to a semi-crushed state and then stir in the yoghurt and mix well. Serve with fish and chips or grilled scallops.

BAKED EGGS

SERVES 4

100g ham, chopped
4 medium free-range eggs
170g Classic Greek yoghurt
salt and freshly ground black pepper

Preheat the oven to 160°C/gas mark 3. Divide the chopped ham between 4 ramekins, then crack an egg into each one and spoon over the yoghurt. Season well and bake for 10 minutes, or until the whites of the eggs are cooked through but the yolks are still soft.

FETA AND CHILLI SPREAD

SERVES 4

150g feta, crumbled
170g Classic Greek yoghurt
1 teaspoon dried chilli flakes

Mix all the ingredients together in a small bowl. This is delicious spread on toasted sourdough bread.

SWEET CHILLI DIP

SERVES 4

170g 0% Greek yoghurt
100ml sweet chilli sauce
1 tablespoon chopped coriander

Mix all the ingredients together in a small bowl. This is great served with potato wedges.

PEANUT BUTTER AND CHILLI SAUCE

SERVES 4

170g 2% Greek yoghurt
100g crunchy peanut butter
50ml sweet chilli sauce
salt and freshly ground black pepper

Mix the yoghurt, peanut butter and chilli sauce together in a small bowl. Season to taste. Serve as an alternative to satay sauce.

HEARTY KALE AND BUTTER BEAN SOUP

This is a hearty and healthy soup for a cold winter's day. Beans are great as they are a combo of proteins and carbs and are also slow releasing. Kale is the green of the season – it's full of iron and nutrients and is a great addition to soups and stews.

SERVES 4

spray oil
1 onion, diced
1 celery stick, diced
1 carrot, peeled and diced
½ sprig of thyme
1 garlic clove, crushed
400g can butter beans, rinsed and drained
500ml hot vegetable stock
100g curly kale, chopped
50g Classic Greek yoghurt
salt and freshly ground black pepper
warm crusty bread, to serve

Spray some oil in a large saucepan and fry the onion, celery, carrot and thyme together over a low heat for about 8–10 minutes until soft.

Add the garlic, butter beans and vegetable stock to the pan. Bring to the boil, then reduce the heat and simmer, uncovered, for approximately 20 minutes until the beans are softened.

Stir in the kale and cook the soup for a further 10 minutes, until the kale is wilted and soft.

Ladle half the soup into a food processor or blender and blitz until smooth. Pour the whizzed soup back into the pan with the rest of the soup. Stir over a medium heat to warm through. Transfer the soup to 4 warmed bowls, place a spoonful of yoghurt in the middle of each bowl, season to taste and serve with warm crusty bread.

TO SPICE UP THE SOUP A LITTLE, TRY STIRRING IN SOME PAN-FRIED CHORIZO BEFORE SERVING

CLASSIC BORSCHT

 Borscht has been a favourite soup of mine for years. It has real depth of flavour if made well and is great for a winter lunch or dinner. Beetroot is such a good ingredient too – it's great for liver cleansing and the colour just brightens everything up (including clothes, so be careful!). The Greek yoghurt is essential here – you really need the creaminess to melt through.

SERVES 4–6

700g pork spare ribs
500g piece of bacon or pancetta
1 large onion
1 large bay leaf
4 allspice berries
4 black peppercorns
3 large carrots, diced
1 large celery stick, chopped
2 teaspoons salt
5 medium beetroots, scrubbed
¼ red cabbage, finely sliced
2 teaspoons granulated sugar
2 tablespoons white wine vinegar
handful of fresh flat-leaf parsley, chopped
salt and freshly ground black pepper
170g Classic Greek yoghurt, to serve

In a large pan, place the spare ribs, bacon or pancetta, whole onion, bay leaf, allspice, black peppercorns, carrots, celery and salt and add enough cold water to cover.

Bring to a boil, then reduce the heat, cover and simmer for about 1–1½ hours or until the spare ribs and bacon or pancetta are tender. Skim any froth that rises to the surface.

Meanwhile, in a separate large pan, cover the beetroot with cold water. Bring to a boil, reduce the heat, cover and simmer for 30 minutes or until the beetroots are tender. Drain well and cover with cold water and let cool for 10 minutes. Peel and grate the beetroots (preferably wearing gloves to avoid staining your skin) and then set aside.

When the spare ribs and bacon or pancetta are tender, remove them from the pan, along with the whole onion, bay leaf, allspice, black peppercorns, carrots and celery. Keep the liquor warm.

Strip the meat off the spare ribs and roughly chop the bacon or pancetta. Return the meat to the pan with the liquor. Add the grated beetroots and red cabbage to the pan and simmer for a further 20 minutes.

Add the sugar, vinegar and parsley to the pan and bring back to the boil, simmer for 5 more minutes, then season to taste. Ladle into soup bowls and serve with a dollop of yoghurt.

CHILLED AVOCADO AND YOGHURT SOUP

I am a bit obsessed with avocados. They lend a silky smoothness to everything they are combined with and this soup is no exception. I also love their pale, elegant green. This soup is a cooling bowl for summer evenings. I won't harp on about the good fats and proteins, as I am sure you've heard it before, but it's right up there in the health stakes, too.

SERVES 4

3 large ripe avocados, halved and stoned
juice of 1 lime
500ml semi-skimmed milk
500g 0% Greek yoghurt
1 tablespoon freshly chopped coriander, plus extra
    to garnish
few drops of Tabasco sauce, to taste
ground cayenne pepper, to garnish
salt and freshly ground black pepper
salted tortilla chips, to serve

Peel and chop the avocados into chunks, then place into a food processor. Pour over the lime juice, add the milk, yoghurt and coriander and process until smooth. Season to taste with Tabasco sauce, salt and freshly ground black pepper.

Refrigerate the soup for at least 2 hours before serving. Place four soup bowls in the fridge to chill.

To serve, divide the soup between the chilled bowls and garnish with fresh coriander and cayenne pepper. Serve with tortilla chips.

BLOODY MARY CHILLED SOUP

 A good Bloody Mary can be a real reviving tonic; a bad one is very disappointing. This soup is like a super-charged Bloody Mary/gazpacho in one. Serve it chilled on a summer's day with a little swirl of Greek yoghurt. It's obviously fab for a hangover, too, but only works if you know the day before that you are heading in that direction due to the overnight straining part. When you get into the habit of making it, a jug will keep in the fridge for a few days and it's equally great without the vodka.

SERVES 4

FOR THE SOUP
1kg ripe plum tomatoes, roughly chopped
1 cucumber, roughly chopped
2 red chillies, chopped and deseeded
1 garlic clove, peeled
3 tablespoons sherry vinegar
2 red peppers, deseeded and roughly chopped
1 teaspoon sea salt
1 teaspoon caster sugar
small bunch of basil
2 tablespoons Worcestershire sauce
1 tablespoon vodka
salt and freshly ground black pepper

FOR THE SALSA
100g cherry tomatoes, quartered
1 tablespoon diced red onion
1 red chilli, deseeded and diced
small handful of basil
100g 0% Greek yoghurt
extra-virgin olive oil, to serve

Place all the soup ingredients in a food processor and blitz until very fine. Chill in the fridge overnight.

Strain the chilled mixture through a sieve over a large mixing bowl. Check the seasoning and the acidity: you want a touch of spice coming through and a lot of the flavour here depends on the ripeness of the ingredients.

To make the salsa, mix the quartered cherry tomatoes, red onion, chilli and basil together in a small dish. Season to taste.

Divide the soup between 4 bowls and place some salsa in the centre of each one. Add enough cold water to the yoghurt to form a pouring consistency. Drizzle the yoghurt over the soup and finish with a dash of olive oil to serve.

MAIN

ROASTED ROOT VEGETABLE SALAD

Everyone raves about getting the right number of portions of fruit and veg a day, but so often people just see vegetables as the boiled side dish of a main meal. Vegetables, when put together well, can form the bulk of many a meal and, if trying to lose weight, making them the main event is a good habit to get into. A salad like this is a great example – and it's equally good served with a turkey steak or roast chicken.

SERVES 4

FOR THE SALAD
1 small celeriac, cut into 2cm chunks
2 carrots, cut into 2cm chunks
2 parsnips, cut into 2cm chunks
2 tablespoons olive oil
3 medium beetroots, cut into 1.5cm thick wedges
2 teaspoons coriander seeds
1½ teaspoons cumin seeds
1 teaspoon fennel seeds
a pinch of salt flakes
15g fresh flat-leaf parsley, roughly chopped
100g radicchio leaves
25g pistachios, shelled and chopped

FOR THE DRESSING
100g Classic Greek yoghurt
1 teaspoon runny honey
1 red chilli, deseeded and finely chopped
juice of ½ lemon
salt and freshly ground black pepper

Preheat the oven to 220°C/gas mark 7. Line a large baking tray with baking parchment.

Toss the celeriac, carrots and parsnips with 1½ tablespoons of the oil and scatter over two-thirds of the baking tray. Mix the beetroots with the remaining oil and add to the remaining one-third of the tray, keeping it separate from the other vegetables to prevent its colour staining them. Roast for 30 minutes.

Coarsely grind the spices with the salt in a pestle and mortar. Add to the vegetables, stirring gently, trying not to mix the beetroot in too much, and roast for a further 30 minutes until the vegetables are tender. Cool for 15 minutes or completely if making ahead.

To make the dressing, mix together the yoghurt, honey, chilli and lemon juice and season.

Place the parsley and radicchio in a large serving bowl, add the roasted vegetables and toss gently. Drizzle the dressing over and scatter with the pistachios.

BRAISED GREEN LENTILS AND RICE WITH CRISPY FRIED ONIONS

 I eat a huge amount of meat and am very pro a high-protein diet, but this is a meat-free dish I often eat for lunch. It's really moreish and I crave it when I want a simple, clean meal. The yoghurt and lentils are a great source of protein and the dish is delicately spiced. You can find all sorts of versions of this recipe and they eat it all over the Middle East. In Lebanon it would be part of the meze, but in Persian cooking it's often served with a fragrant, herb-rich stew as a main.

SERVES 4

200g dried green lentils
25g butter
50ml olive oil
2 onions, finely diced
1 teaspoon ground cumin
300g basmati rice, rinsed
600ml hot vegetable stock
freshly chopped flat-leaf parsley, to garnish
sea salt and freshly ground black pepper
2% Greek yoghurt, to serve

Rinse the lentils, then place in a saucepan and cover with cold water. Bring to the boil and simmer for about 30 minutes until tender. Drain and rinse under cold water.

Meanwhile, in a separate saucepan, heat the butter and the oil, then add the onions and cook over a medium heat for about 20 minutes until deep golden brown. Remove half the onions and set aside.

Add the cumin and rice to the pan and stir well. Pour in the stock and the cooked lentils, season and cover with a tight-fitting lid. Cook for 20 minutes or until all the stock has been absorbed, then fork the grains through, replace the lid and allow to stand, off the heat, for 10 minutes.

To serve, spoon the rice and lentils onto a platter, sprinkle with the reserved onions and garnish with the parsley. Serve with a large dollop of yoghurt.

ROASTED AUBERGINE AND CAULIFLOWER WITH SUMAC AND POMEGRANATE

 This dish reminds me of Beirut. In the Med, so much of your meal is made up of vegetable dishes – it's healthy, economical and always seasonal too. The best meals for me are a couple of protein dishes and then lots of veggies, all served family-style in the middle of the table. This is one of the those dishes. It's great by itself, but I love it with a platter of slow-roasted lamb shoulder too.

SERVES 4

1 cauliflower, broken into small florets
1 aubergine, cut into large chunks
100ml olive oil
large handful of fresh flat-leaf parsley,
   roughly chopped
seeds from 1 pomegranate (or 100g seeds)
bunch of spring onions, finely sliced
1 teaspoon ground sumac
sea salt and freshly ground black pepper

FOR THE DRESSING
170g Classic Greek yoghurt
1 garlic clove, finely chopped
1 teaspoon ground sumac
juice of 1 lemon

Preheat the oven to 180°C/gas mark 4.

Place the cauliflower florets and aubergine chunks in a large bowl, add the olive oil, season and mix well. Place the vegetables on a baking tray or in a roasting tin and roast for about 40 minutes until golden and cooked through. Remove from the oven and set aside to cool.

Meanwhile, mix all the dressing ingredients together and stir in 50ml cold water.

Arrange the aubergine and cauliflower on a platter, then sprinkle over the parsley, pomegranate seeds, spring onions and sumac. Drizzle the dressing over and serve.

BAKED RED PEPPER AND CHILLI EGGS

 This is a breakfast dish that I have been having for years in Greece. When you live there, there are certain ingredients that you always have in abundance in the summer months and the variations of this dish depend on them. We often fry up some sweet red onions and ripe tomatoes and add some eggs, feta and yoghurt, all served with the local sourdough bread. It feels better for you than a full-on fry-up in the heat, but you still get a good, high-protein, savoury breakfast.

SERVES 4

1 tablespoon olive oil
2 red peppers, quartered, deseeded and cut
    into strips
2 yellow peppers, quartered, deseeded and cut
    into strips
1 white onion, halved and finely sliced
2 garlic cloves, sliced
1 red chilli, deseeded and finely diced
200g can chopped tomatoes
4 medium free-range eggs
4 slices of sourdough bread
100g feta, crumbled
170g Classic Greek yoghurt
sea salt and freshly ground black pepper
freshly chopped flat-leaf parsley, to serve

Heat the olive oil in a medium non-stick frying pan with a heatproof handle. Add the peppers, onion and garlic and all but 1 teaspoon of the chopped chilli. Cook over a medium heat until the peppers and onion are softened, but be careful not to burn them. Add the tomatoes, cook for about 20 minutes, then season.

Make 4 equal-sized indentations in the tomato mixture and crack an egg into each one, then cook on the hob for 4 minutes over a medium heat.

Preheat the grill to high. Grill the bread on both sides until toasted. Then remove from the grill and sprinkle the feta over the tomato and egg mixture and spoon the yoghurt between the eggs. Grill for 5 minutes until the eggs are just set.

Transfer the eggs to 4 serving plates and serve with the toast on the side and a sprinkling of the remaining chilli and some chopped parsley over the top.

SMOKED CHEDDAR, GRUYÈRE AND MOZZARELLA MACARONI CHEESE

 Mac and cheese is serious comfort food and super-rich. There is nothing wrong with that, but I do sometimes like to mix it up, and the tanginess of the yoghurt is great here. It does bring down the calories a bit too, but that's not really the drive behind it. The smoked Cheddar and rosemary add more flavour.

SERVES 4

100ml double cream
500ml milk (any type)
1 onion, quartered
1 bay leaf
600g dried macaroni
150g butter, plus extra for greasing
150g plain white flour
250g smoked Cheddar, grated
110g Gruyère, grated
1 tablespoon Dijon mustard
1 tablespoon chopped fresh rosemary
pinch of freshly ground nutmeg
150g mozzarella, diced
170g Classic Greek yoghurt
salt and freshly ground black pepper
watercress salad, to serve

Pour the cream and milk into a small pan and add the onion and bay leaf. Warm through gently over a medium heat. Remove from the heat and set aside to infuse at room temperature for 30 minutes.

Bring a large pan of salted water to the boil and cook the macaroni according to the packet instructions. Drain and set aside to cool.

Preheat the oven to 180°C/gas mark 4. Grease a 15 x 30cm baking dish with butter.

For the sauce, melt the butter in large pan, add the flour and mix well. Cook for 3 minutes over a low heat, stirring constantly to make a smooth paste. Gradually add the infused milk and cream mixture, discarding the onion and bay leaf, stirring well after each addition to prevent any lumps forming.

Stir in half the Cheddar and all the Gruyère, Dijon mustard, rosemary and nutmeg and season with salt and pepper. Add the cold pasta to the cheese sauce and stir well to coat. Fold in the mozzarella pieces and yoghurt.

Pour the mixture into the prepared baking dish, top with the remaining Cheddar and bake for 30 minutes. Serve with a peppery watercress salad.

SLOW-COOKED BOSTON BEANS WITH MUSTARD MASH

Proper baked beans with a good balance of smoky spices, sweetness and savoury braised pork are amazing. Served here with a mash made creamy with Greek yoghurt and rounded off with wholegrain mustard, this is great suppertime food.

SERVES 4

FOR THE BOSTON BEANS
250g smoked streaky bacon, cubed
500g lean belly pork, cubed
24 small pickling onions, peeled and left whole
sprig of thyme
1 tablespoon smoked paprika
2 x 400g cans haricot beans, rinsed and drained
3 tablespoons tomato purée
50g soft brown sugar
salt and freshly ground black pepper

FOR THE MASH
400g potatoes, such as Maris Piper, peeled and
    chopped into even-sized chunks
100g Classic Greek yoghurt
2 tablespoons English mustard

To make the Boston beans, fry the bacon, pork and onions in a large heavy-based pan for 10 minutes over a medium heat, until golden brown. Add the thyme sprig and smoked paprika, stir well and cook for 1 minute.

Add the beans, tomato purée, sugar and 250ml cold water to the pan, season, stir well and bring to the boil. Reduce the heat and simmer for 40–45 minutes, until tender.

Meanwhile, make the mash. Bring a large pan of water to the boil and boil the potatoes for 15–20 minutes until cooked through. Drain the potatoes and mash them, then stir through the Greek yoghurt and mustard.

Serve the beans with the mash.

GNUDI WITH CREAMY TOMATO AND PECORINO SAUCE

 I have long been intrigued by gnudi, but never tried making them until recently. Gnocchi are one of my favourite things to make, but they can feel quite heavy. Well here come gnudi, an answer to my prayers! They are so light, gorgeous, and creamy, I feel like I've missed out for years. I replaced some of the gnudi mix with Greek yoghurt and it worked so well. The key is to leave the gnudi in the fridge long enough to dry out and develop a crust with the semolina. Then you can cook them and serve with all sorts of sauces. I've chosen a classic tomato sauce here, but sage butter would work well too.

SERVES 4

FOR THE GNUDI
150g fresh ricotta (ricotta from a tub is fine)
100g Classic Greek yoghurt
50g Parmesan, grated
50g Italian '00' flour
few gratings of fresh nutmeg
250g semolina

FOR THE SAUCE
50ml olive oil
2 garlic cloves, sliced
400ml passata
small handful of sage leaves, torn
1 teaspoon caster sugar
100g Classic Greek yoghurt
100g Pecorino cheese, grated
sea salt and freshly ground black pepper

Line a baking tray with greaseproof paper.

In a medium bowl, mix the ricotta, yoghurt and Parmesan together, then add the flour and nutmeg. Stir well to combine.

Pour the semolina in an even layer on a baking tray. Take 1 tablespoon of the gnudi mixture and roll it carefully into a ball, place on the semolina tray, roll to coat in the semolina and transfer to the lined tray. Repeat with all of the mixture to make approximately 12 gnudi. Spoon the excess semolina over the balls.

Refrigerate overnight for the gnudi to soak up the semolina.

To make the sauce, heat the olive oil in a large pan over a medium heat, add the garlic and cook for a couple of minutes (do not burn or overcook). Add the passata, sage, sugar and seasoning. Reduce the heat and simmer, uncovered, for 30 minutes.

Bring a large pan of water to the boil. Carefully scoop the gnudi off the semolina tray and drop into the water. Cook for about 4 minutes, then spoon out and add to the tomato sauce. Carefully stir the yoghurt into the tomato sauce.

Divide the gnudi and sauce between four plates, sprinkle over the pecorino and season to taste with black pepper.

MEDITERRANEAN FISH STEW
WITH SAFFRON AÏOLI

 Fish casserole reminds me of sunny holidays in the South of France and Sardinia. This dish has a rich tomato sauce, laced with chilli and extra-virgin olive oil. In France they serve it with *rouille*, a strong garlic and saffron mayonnaise, but I have lightened it up with a saffron-infused yoghurt sauce. Serve with lots of bread to mop up the sauce.

SERVES 4

FOR THE STEW
100ml extra-virgin olive oil
3 garlic cloves, sliced
½ teaspoon dried chilli flakes
400ml passata
50ml white wine
300g monkfish, cut into medium cubes
200g squid rings
4 raw king prawns, peeled
200g live mussels, scrubbed and beards removed (discard any that stay open when sharply tapped)
200g live clams, scrubbed (discard any that stay open when sharply tapped)
small handful of fresh flat-leaf parsley, chopped
toasted sourdough bread, to serve

FOR THE AÏOLI
½ teaspoon saffron threads
170g Classic Greek yoghurt
100ml extra-virgin olive oil
1 garlic clove, very finely chopped
sea salt and freshly ground pepper

Heat the oil in a large pan and fry the garlic and chilli flakes for 5–8 minutes. Add the passata and white wine and simmer for 20 minutes.

Meanwhile, make the aïoli. Pour 50ml hot water over the saffron threads and set aside to infuse for 15 minutes. Combine the saffron mixture with the yoghurt, olive oil and garlic. Season to taste, transfer to a small serving bowl and set aside.

Add the monkfish, squid and prawns to the stew, and cook for about 5 minutes. Add the mussels and clams to the pan and cook, covered, for 5 minutes. Discard any mussels or clams that do not open. Season, stir and sprinkle over the parsley.

Serve the fish stew with sourdough toast and the aïoli on the side.

AÏOLI IS TYPICALLY MADE WITH MAYONNAISE. BY SWAPPING THE MAYO FOR TOTAL GREEK YOGHURT, YOU'VE JUST REDUCED THE CALORIES IN THIS DISH BY OVER 1,000 KCALS

CRAB AND PEA RISOTTO

 Italians are very particular about risottos, as am I. In Italy you would never put cheese in a fish or seafood risotto and I agree, but I do like experimenting, and the addition of Greek yoghurt here is lovely – it adds tanginess and lightens up the dish. I use Vialone Nano rice from the Veneto region – it's a shorter grain and keeps its bite more. Also, seafood and fish risottos are often served in the Veneto area, so this ties in well.

SERVES 4

400ml hot vegetable stock
25g butter
2 tablespoons olive oil
1 onion, finely chopped
2 garlic cloves, finely chopped
200g risotto rice
100ml white wine
200g frozen peas, defrosted
200g white crab meat
small handful of chopped chives
zest of 1 lemon
50g Classic Greek yoghurt
sea salt and freshly ground black pepper
peashoots, to garnish (optional)

Pour the stock into a saucepan and bring to the boil, then reduce to a simmer.

Meanwhile, heat the butter and oil in a medium, deep, non-stick frying pan over a medium heat, then add the onion and garlic and cook for 5 minutes until softened and translucent. Add the risotto rice and stir to coat with the oil.

Pour in the wine and stir until it is all absorbed, then add a ladleful of the hot stock and stir until it is fully absorbed into the rice. Continue to add the stock, ladleful by ladleful, stirring the rice to absorb the stock after each addition. This will take 30–40 minutes in total. About 35 minutes into the rice cooking time, stir in the peas and crab meat. The rice should still retain a little bite once it is cooked – you may not need to use all of the stock.

When the rice is cooked, stir through the chives, lemon zest and yoghurt and season to taste.

Garnish with peashoots, if desired, and serve.

CRAB LINGUINE

 In Italy, each pasta shape has its purpose and linguine are really good for seafood dishes. At Pont St, my restaurant, we make a rich creamy bisque sauce with lobster and brandy, but it takes a lot of time and prep. This is a quicker, lighter and healthier version for home, and the brown crab meat gives fantastic flavour.

SERVES 4

400g dried linguine
100ml extra-virgin olive oil
1 red chilli, deseeded and finely chopped
4 garlic cloves, finely chopped
25ml brandy
200g brown crab meat
200g white crab meat
handful of fresh flat-leaf parsley
100g Classic Greek yoghurt
salt and freshly ground black pepper

Bring a large pan of water to the boil and cook the linguine according to the packet instructions.

In a large, non-stick frying pan, heat the oil and gently fry the chilli and garlic for 5–8 minutes. Then add the brandy and cook for 5 minutes. Remove from the heat and stir in the brown and white crab meat, parsley and yoghurt.

Drain the pasta, add to the sauce, stir well, season to taste and serve.

A MORE DECADENT VERSION OF THIS PASTA DISH MIGHT USE CREAM RATHER THAN TOTAL GREEK YOGHURT, BUT DOING SO WOULD INCREASE YOUR CALORIE INTAKE BY APPROXIMATELY 350KCALS

PAN-FRIED SALMON WITH CUCUMBER AND DILL SALAD

 Pan-fried salmon, waxy new potatoes and cool yoghurt, cucumber and dill salad is really simplicity at its best. The salad can be made a few hours ahead and kept in the fridge, then the salmon and potatoes get cooked up when you are ready to go.

SERVES 4

300g new potatoes
1 medium cucumber, peeled and finely sliced
170g Classic Greek yoghurt
small bunch of fresh dill, finely chopped
juice of 1 lemon, or to taste
1 tablespoon olive oil
4 x 200g salmon steaks
sea salt

Place the potatoes in a medium pan, cover with salted water, bring to the boil and simmer for 20 minutes until just cooked. Drain.

Place the cucumber slices in a bowl, rub 1 teaspoon sea salt into the slices and leave for 5 minutes. Rinse the salt off the cucumber under cold running water, then pat dry with kitchen paper. Mix the cucumber with the yoghurt, dill and a squeeze of lemon. Chill in the fridge.

Heat the oil in a medium, non-stick frying pan over a medium heat and sear the salmon for about 4 minutes on each side, depending on its thickness. It should be pink in the middle and golden on the outside.

Serve the salmon with the new potatoes and cucumber salad.

FOR A HEALTHIER OPTION, SIMPLY COOK THE FISH FOR 5 MINUTES ON EACH SIDE UNDER A GRILL RATHER THAN BATTERING AND FRYING IT

FISH TACOS, CHIPOTLE YOGHURT AND PICKLED RED ONIONS

 American food is enjoying a real resurgence right now. It's all about old favourites with a simple, gourmet twist and these fish tacos are the perfect example. Crispy, hot fish, spicy yoghurt and pickled red onions are a fantastic combination.

SERVES 4

FOR THE PICKLED ONIONS
300ml white wine vinegar
100g caster sugar
2 red onions, finely sliced

FOR THE CHIPOTLE YOGHURT
170g 0% Greek yoghurt
50g chipotle chilli paste or 50g canned chipotles, drained and chopped
sea salt and freshly ground black pepper

FOR THE FISH
100g plain white flour
150ml sparkling water
150ml sunflower or vegetable oil
800g skinned white fish (eg cod or hake), cut into bite-size pieces

TO SERVE
½ iceberg lettuce, shredded
8 small soft wheat tortillas
finely chopped coriander leaves
4 lime wedges

To make the pickled onions, place the vinegar and sugar in a small pan. Bring to the boil, then reduce the heat and simmer for a couple of minutes. Remove from the heat, add the finely sliced onions, and set aside to cool.

For the chipotle yoghurt, blitz or stir together the yoghurt and chipotle paste or chopped chipotle, then season to taste and set aside.

To make the batter for the fish, mix together the flour and sparkling water in a large shallow bowl. Heat the oil for a few minutes in a large sauté pan over a medium heat, being careful to not let it get too hot (you can test to see if it is hot enough by dropping in a piece of bread – it should sizzle). Quickly dip the fish in the batter to coat lightly and then fry in the oil, in batches if necessary, for a couple of minutes on each side. Remove with a slotted spoon and drain on kitchen paper.

To serve, place a little shredded lettuce in each tortilla, top with some fish, a dollop of chipotle yoghurt and a spoonful of pickled onions, and fold in half to make a soft-shell taco. Serve with a scattering of coriander and a wedge of fresh lime on the side.

SMOKED HADDOCK BREAKFAST FLORENTINE

Everyone loves eggs Florentine, and having a high protein breakfast, with the addition of spinach, is a great way to start the day. I find Hollandaise sauce too rich in the morning, though, so here we have made eggs Florentine with some lovely smoked haddock and topped it with creamy yoghurt instead.

SERVES 2

200g dyed smoked haddock
600ml milk (any type)
2 English muffins
bunch of fresh chives
200g Classic Greek yoghurt
200g baby spinach
2 tablespoons white wine vinegar
2 medium free-range eggs
salt and freshly ground black pepper
lemon wedges, to serve

Place the smoked haddock in a medium pan, add the milk and poach over a low heat for approximately 8–10 minutes, bringing it to a simmer. Remove the cooked haddock from the milk, reserving the flavoured milk. Cool and flake the fish.

Cut the muffins in half and toast.

Snip three-quarters of the chives and mix into the yoghurt along with 75ml of the reserved milk. Season with salt and pepper.

Wilt the spinach gently in a medium, non-stick frying pan over a low heat for about 5 minutes. Drain off any excess liquid.

Meanwhile, fill a small saucepan three-quarters full with cold water. Add the vinegar and bring to the boil. Carefully break in the eggs and poach for approximately 2½ minutes to keep the yolk runny.

Divide the spinach between the muffins, top each with half the flaked haddock and a poached egg. Drizzle with the yoghurt dressing. Serve with lemon wedges and scatter with the reserved chives.

FOR A VEGETARIAN VERSION, THE SMOKED HADDOCK CAN BE REPLACED WITH MUSHROOMS SAUTÉED IN BUTTER

STEAMED GARLIC MUSSELS

 Simple and classic. Mussels are one of the best forms of protein and also quick and cheap to prepare. I love picking through mussels and slurping up the liquid afterwards – it's a fantastically involved meal and always makes me happy.

SERVES 4

100g butter
2 shallots, finely sliced
4 garlic cloves, finely sliced
1kg live mussels, scrubbed and beards removed (discard any that stay open when sharply tapped)
100ml white wine
handful of fresh flat-leaf parsley, chopped
100g Classic Greek yoghurt
freshly ground black pepper

Melt the butter in a large pan and fry the shallots and garlic for about 5 minutes or until translucent. Remove the shallots and garlic from the pan using a slotted spoon and set aside.

Heat the pan to a high heat and add the mussels and wine, cover and steam for 5 minutes. Discard any mussels that do not open. Return the shallots and garlic to the pan, then add the parsley and yoghurt, season with black pepper, mix well and serve.

PRAWN NOODLE SALAD WITH SPICY PEANUT DRESSING

When I really feel like being healthy and eating a super 'clean' plate of food, something like a Thai-inspired noodle dish is perfect. The yoghurt adds protein and creaminess for a boost.

SERVES 2

FOR THE SALAD
100g rice noodles
125g frozen soya beans
200g cooked, peeled king prawns
½ medium mango, cut into thin strips
4 spring onions, thinly sliced on the diagonal
½ cucumber, halved, deseeded and sliced
small bunch of fresh coriander, roughly torn
salad leaves, to serve

FOR THE DRESSING
1 red chilli, deseeded and finely chopped
zest of 1 and juice of 2 limes
2 tablespoons smooth peanut butter
2 tablespoons soy sauce
4 tablespoons 0% Greek yoghurt

Bring a pan of water to the boil and cook the noodles according to the packet instructions.

At the end of the noodle cooking time add the soya beans to the pan and turn off the heat. Leave for 1 minute, then drain and rinse under cold running water. Drain again and transfer to a large serving bowl.

Add the prawns, mango, spring onions, cucumber and coriander to the bowl and stir well to combine with the noodles and beans.

To make the dressing, whisk together the chilli, lime juice and zest, peanut butter and soy sauce in a small bowl until smooth. Add the yoghurt and stir well. Drizzle over the salad and toss before serving with salad leaves.

INDIAN SPICED MONKFISH WITH SPINACH, LENTIL AND YOGHURT DAHL

Monkfish is a great fish for Indian-inspired dishes. It holds its shape well and works with bold flavours. The yoghurt is a cooling agent in this dish and works beautifully.

SERVES 2

2 x 200g monkfish tails
1 teaspoon garam masala or curry powder
2 tablespoons vegetable oil
1 teaspoon cumin seeds
1 teaspoon saffron threads
¾ teaspoon ground turmeric
1 onion, chopped
2 garlic cloves, chopped
3 red or green chillies, deseeded and chopped
2 teaspoons tomato purée
400g can green lentils, rinsed and drained
400g baby spinach
15g coriander, freshly chopped
200g Classic Greek yoghurt
salt and freshly ground black pepper

Roll the monkfish in half of the garam masala or curry powder. Season and then pan fry over a medium heat for 8–10 minutes, turning to cook both sides.

Heat the oil in a separate large pan over a medium heat. Add the cumin seeds, saffron, the remaining garam masala or curry powder, the turmeric, onion, garlic and chillies and cook for 8 minutes. Add the tomato purée and lentils and cook for a further 5 minutes. Add the monkfish and cook for another 5 minutes. Stir in the spinach and coriander until wilted. Remove from heat, then stir in the yoghurt.

Divide the spinach and lentil mixture between two plates, arrange the monkfish on top and serve.

SMOKED HADDOCK AND PRAWN PILAF WITH CORIANDER AND CASHEW YOGHURT

This is a recipe from the Total Greek Yoghurt archives. I was attracted to it because it's a bit like a pimped-up kedgeree. I think the idea of the yoghurt thickened and flavoured with the cashews is great too.

SERVES 4

FOR THE PILAF

4 medium free-range eggs
large pinch of saffron threads
450ml hot fish stock
2 tablespoons sunflower oil
1 large onion, finely chopped
2 teaspoons ground coriander
1 teaspoon cumin seeds
1–2 green chillies, deseeded and thinly sliced
175g basmati rice, rinsed well in cold water
    and drained
350g smoked haddock, skinned, boned and cut
    into 3cm chunks
175g raw, peeled large king prawns

FOR THE CASHEW YOGHURT

40g cashews, finely chopped
150g 0% Greek yoghurt
15g coriander, freshly chopped
zest and juice of ½ lemon or 1 lime

Boil the eggs in water for 8 minutes until hard boiled. Set aside to cool. Once cooled, peel and quarter the eggs.

Mix the saffron with the hot stock and set aside for 10 minutes.

Heat the oil in a large, wide, non-stick frying or sauté pan over a medium heat. Add the onion, ground coriander, cumin and chillies and fry for 10 minutes until golden.

Add the rice and stock with the saffron threads to the pan, bring to the boil, stir well and cover. Reduce to a gentle simmer and cook for 8 minutes.

Meanwhile, make the cashew yoghurt. Dry-fry the cashews in a small non-stick frying pan over a medium heat until golden, cool for a few minutes, then mix with the yoghurt, coriander and lemon or lime zest and juice.

Gently stir the rice, scatter the haddock and prawns on the top, cover again and cook for a further 8 minutes, until the fish and prawns are cooked through.

Serve the pilaf with the coriander and cashew yoghurt.

TOTAL +3

Total Greek Yoghurt is a fantastically versatile ingredient to use in sauces, dressings and dips. With the addition of just a few simple ingredients, you can use your yoghurt to create something that tastes much better than the readymade dressings and dips you'll find in the supermarket. All of these recipes will transform your yoghurt with the addition of just 3 ingredients.

BLUE CHEESE DIP

SERVES 4

splash of olive oil
2 banana shallots, finely diced
300g Classic Greek yoghurt
200g soft blue cheese (Danish blue or Roquefort)

Heat the olive oil in a medium non-stick frying pan and fry the shallots until translucent. Add the yoghurt, crumble in the blue cheese and stir over a low heat so that the cheese warms through but doesn't melt completely.

SRIRACHA CHILLI AND LIME SAUCE

SERVES 4

170g Classic Greek yoghurt
50ml Sriracha chilli sauce or a hot spicy sauce alternative
zest and juice of ½ lime
1 teaspoon chopped coriander
salt and freshly ground black pepper

Mix all the ingredients together in a small bowl and season to taste. Serve with Asian-inspired salads or as an alternative to prawn cocktail sauce.

HONEY AND TAHINI DRESSING

SERVES 4

170g Classic Greek yoghurt
1 tablespoon runny honey
1 tablespoon tahini
1 garlic clove, crushed
salt and freshly ground black pepper

Mix all the ingredients together in a small bowl. Season to taste and then stir in a little cold water to thin the dressing to your preferred consistency.

RANCH DRESSING

SERVES 4

170g Classic Greek yoghurt
2 tablespoons chopped mixed herbs (eg chives and parsley)
1 garlic clove, crushed
50ml lemon juice
sea salt and freshly ground black pepper

Mix all the ingredients together, then stir in a little cold water to thin it to your preferred consistency.

BEETROOT TZATZIKI

SERVES 4

100g cooked beetroots, finely grated
170g Classic Greek yoghurt
2 garlic cloves, crushed
1 tablespoon chopped mint
salt and freshly ground black pepper

Place the beetroot in a sieve and press out the excess liquid using the back of a spoon. Transfer the beetroot to a small serving dish and mix in the remaining ingredients, season to taste and chill.

CLASSIC TZATZIKI

SERVES 4

½ teaspoon salt
½ cucumber, coarsely grated
170g Classic Greek yoghurt
2 garlic cloves, finely chopped
1 tablespoon chopped mint

Stir the salt into the cucumber and set aside for 30 minutes.

Place the cucumber in a sieve and press out the excess liquid using the back of a spoon. Mix the cucumber with the yoghurt, garlic and mint, then chill.

POTATO RÖSTI AND SMOKED SALMON WITH VODKA-SPIKED YOGHURT AND SALMON KETA

 Brunch is one of the best meals of the week: slow, lazy eating, big flavours for breakfast if you've woken up late or a light dish for your lunch if you're an early bird. This is a blinder – crisp rösti, smoked salmon and punchy yoghurt topping. Really good.

SERVES 4, AS A STARTER OR BRUNCH DISH

FOR THE RÖSTI AND SALMON
2 medium floury potatoes, such as Maris Piper, unpeeled and scrubbed
25g Classic Greek yoghurt
50ml olive oil
25g butter
200g smoked salmon, sliced
2 spring onions, finely sliced
100g salmon keta (large salmon eggs)
sea salt and freshly ground black pepper

FOR THE VODKA-SPIKED YOGHURT
170g Classic Greek yoghurt
2 tablespoons vodka
zest of ½ lemon

Preheat the oven to 180°C/gas mark 4.

Grate the potatoes and squeeze out the excess liquid by gently squeezing them in a clean tea towel. Transfer the potato to a medium bowl and stir in the yoghurt. Season and stir well to combine.

To make the vodka-spiked yoghurt, mix the yoghurt, vodka and lemon zest together in a small serving dish. Season to taste and set aside.

Heat the olive oil and butter in a medium, non-stick frying pan. Divide the potato mixture into 8 equal portions and shape into rounds using your hands. Fry a couple of the rösti at a time, for 5 minutes on each side or until golden brown. Transfer to a baking tray and keep hot in the oven. Repeat to cook the remaining röstis.

To serve, place two röstis on each plate and top with the smoked salmon, vodka yoghurt, sliced spring onions and finally the salmon eggs.

SPINACH, BUTTERNUT SQUASH AND FETA QUESADILLAS

 These are a great snack and a good way for kids to get their veggie quota, whilst being tasty enough to serve to adults too. They have a bit of a Greek pastry feel to them and are very moreish.

SERVES 4

400g diced, peeled butternut squash
1 tablespoon olive oil
150g cooked spinach, roughly chopped
4 spring onions, finely sliced
200g feta, crumbled
170g Classic Greek yoghurt
8 flour tortillas
sea salt and freshly ground black pepper

Preheat the oven to 180°C/gas mark 4. Put the diced butternut squash in a roasting tin, coat with the oil and roast for about 30 minutes.

Mix the spinach, spring onions, feta, roasted squash and yoghurt together in a bowl and season to taste.

Take a tortilla and lay it flat on a board. Place about 3 dessertspoonfuls of the squash and spinach mixture on half of the tortilla, then fold it in half.

Heat up a griddle pan and char the quesadilla on each side, for about 10 minutes in total. Repeat with the remaining tortillas. Finally, pop them in the oven for 10 minutes, cut into smaller pieces and serve.

CLUB SANDWICHES

Club sandwiches are great, but I hate them when they are filled with goopy mayonnaise. In this great Total Yoghurt archive recipe, Greek yoghurt is used instead for a lighter, fresher feel.

SERVES 4

2 chicken breasts
8 rashers streaky smoked bacon
2 tablespoons Classic Greek yoghurt
2 teaspoons wholegrain mustard
12 slices of your favourite bread
4 medium free-range eggs
4–6 Bibb or Little Gem lettuce leaves
1 avocado, halved, stoned and sliced
2 ripe tomatoes, sliced
salt and freshly ground black pepper

Preheat the oven to 200°C/gas mark 6. Season the chicken breasts, place on a baking tray, cover with foil and cook in the oven for about 15 minutes. Set aside to cool, then slice.

Grill or fry the bacon for about 6 minutes on each side, until crispy.

Combine the yoghurt with the mustard in a small bowl.

When you are ready to eat, toast the bread and then pan fry the eggs to your liking in a non-stick frying pan.

Then layer it up! For each sandwich, start with a slice of toast, spread with some yogurt mixture, then top with chicken, lettuce, avocado and tomato. Top with another slice of toast, spread with more yoghurt and pile on one fried egg and two slices of bacon. Then top with the final slice of toast. Cut into four, secure with wooden skewers and serve.

BY REPLACING THE MAYONNAISE USUALLY FOUND IN A CLUB SANDWICH WITH TOTAL GREEK YOGHURT, YOU'VE REDUCED THE FAT IN THIS DISH BY 94%

PRESERVED LEMON AND YOGHURT-MARINATED POUSSINS

 This is a barbecue recipe through and through: gorgeously flavoursome, overnight-marinated chicken. I like the smaller chickens for this recipe, as they take on the flavours and barbecue well. Also, they cook much faster. Preserved lemons are used a lot in Moroccan food – they are good blitzed with some honey and chilli as I've done in this marinade, giving a lot of flavour for not much effort. They can be found in many supermarkets too.

SERVES 4

4 poussins, spatchcocked

FOR THE MARINADE

3 preserved lemons, drained
2 garlic cloves
2 shallots
3 tablespoons runny honey
1 teaspoon dried chilli flakes
small handful of fresh thyme
100g Classic Greek yoghurt
salt and freshly ground black pepper

FOR THE SALAD

1 red onion
200g cherry tomatoes
2 baby cucumbers
100ml extra-virgin olive oil
100g green cracked olives
1 lemon, cut into wedges
170g Classic Greek yoghurt
1 tablespoon za'atar
flatbreads, to serve (optional)

Mix all the marinade ingredients together, then blitz in a blender. Place the poussins in a large airtight container, rub the marinade all over, seal with the lid and chill overnight in the fridge.

To cook on the barbecue, heat your barbecue to white coal stage. Cook the chicken for about 10–15 minutes on each side.

If cooking in the kitchen, preheat the oven to 220°C/ gas mark 7. Heat a griddle pan over a medium heat. Generously season the poussins and brown on the griddle, in batches if necessary, for about 5 minutes each side. Transfer the poussins to a roasting tin and roast in the oven for 15 minutes.

Whilst the poussins are roasting, chop the onion, tomatoes and cucumbers into cubes and mix with the olive oil, olives and a squeeze of lemon juice.

Place each poussin on a serving plate with a pile of salad, a dollop of the yoghurt and a sprinkling of za'atar, and serve with warm flatbreads.

DUCK KEBABS WITH ROSE RAITA
AND PILAU RICE

 This is probably my favourite recipe in this book. The lightly spiced duck skewers and fragrant rosewater yoghurt raita feel romantic, as Middle Eastern flavours often do. You will need 8 kebab skewers.

SERVES 4

FOR THE DUCK KEBABS
1 teaspoon ground cinnamon
2 teaspoons cumin seeds
1 teaspoon ground coriander
2 teaspoons garam masala
1 tablespoon olive oil
4 duck breasts, skinned and each cut into
    8 equal-sized pieces

FOR THE RAITA
½ teaspoon cumin seeds
½ teaspoon cardamom seeds
170g 0% Greek yoghurt
small handful of chopped mint
2 teaspoons rosewater
1 teaspoon runny honey
salt and freshly ground black pepper

FOR THE PILAU RICE
50g butter
1 onion, finely diced
250g basmati rice, rinsed
pinch of saffron threads
500ml hot vegetable stock

If you are using wooden skewers, soak them in cold water before cooking to prevent them from burning during cooking.

For the kebabs, combine the spices and oil in a large lidded airtight container. Add the duck to the container, stir well, seal with the lid and chill in the fridge for a couple of hours.

For the raita, heat a small non-stick frying pan over a medium heat and gently dry-fry the cumin and cardamom seeds for about 5 minutes, being careful not to burn them. Remove the pan from the heat. Place the yoghurt in a small dish and stir in the seeds, mint, rosewater and honey, then season and set aside.

For the rice, melt the butter in a medium pan, add the onion and cook for about 15 minutes, until golden brown. Then add the rice, stir to coat with the butter, and add the saffron and stock. Bring to the boil, reduce the heat, cover with a lid and simmer for 20 minutes or until all the liquid has evaporated. Leave the lid on for a further 10 minutes, then fluff the rice with a fork.

Meanwhile, heat a griddle pan over a high heat or preheat the grill to high. Thread 4 pieces of duck onto each skewer and cook for approximately 5 minutes on each side – the centre of the meat should still be pink.

To serve, divide the rice between four plates, place the kebabs on top, and serve the raita on the side.

CRISPY YOGHURT-MARINATED CHICKEN WITH RED CABBAGE COLESLAW

 A buttermilk marinade is traditionally used to tenderise chicken pieces before cooking, but Greek yoghurt is also perfect for this. Greek yoghurt is also a great healthy substitute for the mayonnaise in the coleslaw, and it lends the dish a lovely clean, tangy flavour. If you wish to be completely virtuous, you could bake the chicken pieces, but I prefer to shallow fry them, as a little crispiness is just right.

SERVES 4

FOR THE CHICKEN
400g Classic Greek yoghurt
4 free-range chicken drumsticks, skinned
4 free-range chicken thighs, skinned
150g polenta
½ teaspoon garlic granules
½ teaspoon smoked paprika
½ teaspoon dried oregano
50g Parmesan, finely grated
100ml olive oil
sea salt and freshly ground black pepper

FOR THE COLESLAW
400g red cabbage, finely sliced
3 carrots, grated
1 red onion, finely chopped

FOR THE DRESSING
200g 2% Greek yoghurt
1 tablespoon Dijon mustard
1 teaspoon caster sugar
50ml cider vinegar

Place the yoghurt in a large bowl and season. Add the chicken pieces and turn so the meat is completely coated in yoghurt. Cover and leave to marinate overnight if possible, or for at least 2 hours, in the fridge.

To make the coleslaw, place the cabbage, carrots and red onion in a large bowl and toss to combine. In a separate bowl, mix together all the dressing ingredients and then stir this through the coleslaw until evenly distributed.

Preheat the oven to 180°C/gas mark 4.

In a large bowl, mix the polenta, garlic granules, paprika, oregano and Parmesan together. Lift the chicken pieces out of the yoghurt marinade, shaking off any excess, and then roll the meat in the polenta mix to coat each piece on all sides.

Heat the olive oil in a large non-stick frying pan over a medium heat and pan-fry the chicken, in batches if necessary, for approximately 8–10 minutes until golden brown and crispy. Transfer the chicken to a baking tray and cook in the oven for a further 15 minutes.

Place the chicken pieces on a plate lined with kitchen paper to drain, then transfer to serving plates. Serve the crispy chicken with the coleslaw.

HONEYED TURKEY AND AVOCADO SALAD WITH MINT DRESSING

Turkey is a great meat, as it's full of amino acids and zinc and is also very lean. This salad is great for a healthy lunch and the avocado adds healthy fats, too.

SERVES 2

FOR THE SALAD
8 asparagus spears
1 tablespoon runny honey
1 teaspoon soy sauce
300g turkey breast
100g watercress
200g cherry tomatoes, halved
1 avocado, diced
salt and freshly ground black pepper

FOR THE DRESSING
2 tablespoons Classic Greek yoghurt
1 tablespoon chopped mint
juice of 1 lemon

Preheat the grill to high. Place the asparagus on a baking tray and season well. Cook under the grill until tender – this should take about 5 minutes. Leave the grill on for the turkey.

Mix the honey and soy sauce together and pour it over the turkey breast. Grill the turkey for 8 minutes on each side.

For the dressing, combine the yoghurt, mint and lemon juice together and season well.

To serve, divide the asparagus, watercress, tomatoes and avocado between two plates, top with the sliced turkey, and drizzle the dressing over.

PORK LOIN STEAKS WITH MUSHROOMS, SMOKED BACON AND CREAMY APPLE DIP

This recipe is from the Total Greek Yoghurt archives. I picked it because it's really good for when time is limited. The smoky bacon, mushrooms and apples all combine with the yoghurt to create what feels like a very decadent meal, but actually isn't. Good served with the Mustard Mash from page 75.

SERVES 4

4 large pork loin steaks
4 portobello or field mushrooms, left whole
15g butter
4 rashers of smoked bacon, cut into strips
4 sprigs of thyme
4 garlic cloves, sliced
50ml balsamic vinegar
50ml white wine vinegar

FOR THE DIP

2 apples, cored and diced
250g Classic Greek yoghurt
juice of 1 lemon

Cut 8 pieces of foil measuring approximately 30 x 15cm.

Preheat a griddle pan and quickly chargrill the pork steaks to mark the meat with stripes.

Preheat the oven to 200°C/gas mark 6.

Place a pork steak on top of one of the pieces of foil, then place another piece of foil on top. Fold the foil over and then fold over the ends, creating a bag effect. Leave the top of the bag open. Repeat with each steak.

Divide the mushrooms, butter, bacon, thyme, garlic and vinegars equally between the bags.

Fold over the tops to seal and create 4 neat parcels. Place the parcels in a roasting tin and bake for 15–20 minutes.

To make the dip, combine the apples, yoghurt and lemon juice in a bowl.

Remove the contents from the parcels and serve with a big dollop of the apple dip.

TO COOK THE STEAKS ON A BARBECUE, CHARGRILL THE PORK STEAKS ON A HOT BARBECUE UNTIL MARKED WITH STRIPES. THEN PREPARE THE PARCELS AS ABOVE. COOK THE PARCELS ON THE BARBECUE FOR 15–20 MINUTES

PEAR AND CELERIAC REMOULADE WITH PARMA HAM

 Bayonne or Parma ham with remoulade is quite a classic combo, and it's easy to see why – the savoury celeriac, tangy mustard dressing and salty ham are great. I add a pear for a touch of sweetness. You could serve this as a starter if you like, or as a light main with crusty bread.

SERVES 4

1 celeriac, peeled weight approximately 400g
1 medium pear
100g Classic Greek yoghurt
1 tablespoon wholegrain mustard
8 slices of Parma ham
sea salt and freshly ground black pepper
snipped chives, to garnish (optional)
crusty bread, to serve

Bring a large pan of water to the boil. Cut the celeriac into fine, even-sized strips. Blanch the celeriac strips in the boiling water for 2 minutes, drain and cool under cold running water until cold. Drain thoroughly. Cut the pear into similar sized strips.

For the dressing, mix the yoghurt with the mustard in a medium bowl, season and stir in the celeriac and the pear.

To serve, arrange the celeriac salad and Parma ham on a serving plate. Sprinkle with the chives, and serve immediately with crusty bread.

PAPRIKA AND PORK MEATBALLS
IN TOMATO SAUCE

 These are so simple to make, and so loved by everyone. The paprika gives smoky depth and the mixture of pork and beef is great too. The Greek yoghurt is intrinsic to this dish. I prefer this with a bowl of buttered rice, but it is great with noodles too.

SERVES 4

2 onions, grated
4 garlic cloves, finely grated
500g minced beef
500g minced pork
2 teaspoons sweet paprika
1 teaspoon hot paprika
1 teaspoon dried oregano
1 medium free-range egg
1 teaspoon snipped chives
1 teaspoon sea salt
100ml white wine
400g can chopped tomatoes
1 teaspoon caster sugar
2 bay leaves
400g basmati rice
2 knobs of butter
170g Classic Greek yoghurt

Place the onions and garlic in a bowl and squeeze out some of the excess liquid. Add the two meats, the sweet and hot paprikas, dried oregano, egg, chives and salt. Mix really well, combining all the flavours. It should take about 8 minutes to get it all mixed in.

Use your hands to form the mixture into little balls, about 30g each. This will make about 20 meatballs.

Heat a heavy-based, deep, non-stick frying pan over a medium to high heat and seal the meatballs off until golden brown on all sides. This will take about 15 minutes. Season them again and then pour in the white wine and cook for 3 minutes.

Stir in the tomatoes, sugar and bay leaves. Reduce the heat to low and cook for about 30–40 minutes until the sauce is thick and tasty.

Meanwhile, pour the rice into a saucepan and add 400ml cold water. Bring to the boil, cover and simmer for 15–20 minutes until the water has evaporated.

Take the rice off the heat, add a couple of knobs of butter and stir, then leave to sit, covered, for 10 minutes.

When the meatballs are ready, dollop some yoghurt all over the pan, lightly stir in and serve with the buttered rice on the side.

CREAMY BUBBLE AND SQUEAK WITH HAM AND FRIED EGGS

Bubble and squeak is a brilliant British dish. Yes, it's made using leftovers, but it's got a wonderfully daft name and is really tasty!

SERVES 2

knob of butter
1 onion, finely chopped
150g leftover mashed potato or roughly chopped roast potatoes
50g leftover cooked cabbage
50g Classic Greek yoghurt
2 tablespoons olive oil
2 medium free-range eggs
4 slices of thick-cut ham
salt and freshly ground black pepper

Heat the butter in a large, non-stick frying pan and fry the onion for 5–10 minutes or until it is cooked. Add the potatoes and cabbage to the pan. Mix well and add the yoghurt. Transfer to a bowl, season and shape into 2 patties.

Add 1 tablespoon of the olive oil to the pan and fry the patties for 10 minutes on each side or until golden brown.

Meanwhile, heat the remaining olive in a separate pan and fry the eggs to your liking. Serve the patties topped with two slices of ham and a fried egg.

SEARED BEEF WITH MELTING BLUE CHEESE SAUCE

 A classic steak with a creamy blue cheese sauce is hard to beat, especially when made with healthy Greek yoghurt instead of calorie-dense cream and butter. Served with some seasonal green vegetables, this makes a lovely, quick weekend dinner to share with friends.

SERVES 4

4 x 300g thick-cut sirloin steaks
25ml olive oil, plus extra for brushing the steak
200g watercress
sea salt and freshly ground black pepper

FOR THE BLUE CHEESE SAUCE

splash of olive oil
2 banana shallots, finely diced
300g Classic Greek yoghurt
200g soft blue cheese (Danish blue or Roquefort)

Prepare two pans, one for the sauce and one for the steaks. I like to cook steak in a heavy-based cast-iron frying pan, so get one smoking hot whilst you season the meat well and brush it with a little olive oil on both sides. Sear the steaks for about 4 minutes on each side, then remove from the pan and rest for 5 minutes to let the muscles relax and the juices settle. This would leave it medium rare, depending on thickness, so adjust the cooking time according to how you prefer your steak.

Meanwhile, in the second pan, heat the olive oil and fry the shallots until translucent. Add the yoghurt, crumble in the blue cheese and stir over a low heat so that the cheese warms through but doesn't melt completely.

To serve, simply arrange the steak on a pile of watercress, and then top with a big dollop of sauce.

CHIPOTLE TURKEY AND BLACK TURTLE BEAN CHILLI

Turkey is a much maligned meat. It's often dismissed as dry and boring or only for health freaks, but in fact, like anything, it just needs to be cooked properly. It is a superfood packed with zinc and potassium. In this chilli, turkey is a great alternative to beef, both from a health point of view and also just for a change. I always add a bit of cocoa to my chillis too – it really works and adds depth of flavour.

SERVES 4

60g dried black turtle beans, soaked in cold water
    overnight, then drained and rinsed
50ml olive oil
8 skinless, boneless turkey steaks
2 onions, diced
1 large red onion, diced
2 garlic cloves, crushed
1 red chilli, finely chopped and deseeded
    if preferred
400g can baked beans
200g can black-eye beans
1 red pepper, diced
2 teaspoons chipotle chilli paste
100ml passata
1 tablespoon cocoa powder
sea salt and freshly ground black pepper
chopped coriander, to garnish
200g 0% Greek yoghurt, to serve

Boil the turtle beans for 20–25 minutes.

Heat the olive oil in a large, heavy-based pan over a low heat. Gently cook the turkey for approximately 5 minutes, until golden brown. Then add the onions, garlic and chilli and fry for a further 10 minutes.

Add the drained turtle beans and the remaining ingredients, except the cocoa powder, and simmer for a further 30–35 minutes. Then add the cocoa powder, stir and season.

Sprinkle with chopped coriander and serve with the yoghurt.

BALSAMIC GLAZED CHICKEN
WITH FENNEL MASH

The flavours of clementine and fennel really work well together. Chicken is a fail-safe dish and the fennel mash and full flavoured sauce work a treat.

SERVES 2

FOR THE CHICKEN
2 tablespoons balsamic vinegar
1 tablespoon soft brown sugar
2 skinless free-range chicken breasts
250ml chicken stock
250ml clementine juice
2 clementines, segmented
2 tablespoons Classic Greek yoghurt
salt and freshly ground black pepper

FOR THE MASH
2 large potatoes, peeled and chopped
30g butter
1 fennel bulb, chopped
75g Classic Greek yoghurt

Preheat the oven to 200°C /gas mark 6.

Mix together the balsamic vinegar and brown sugar to make a marinade.

Score the chicken breasts, season with salt and pepper and cover with the marinade. Refrigerate for 30 minutes.

Meanwhile, get started on the mash. Boil the potatoes and keep warm.

Remove the chicken from the fridge and place it on a baking tray. Cook in the oven for 12–14 minutes.

Meanwhile, in a saucepan melt the butter over a low–medium heat and gently sweat the fennel until soft and tender.

In a separate pan, bring the chicken stock and clementine juice to the boil and let it reduce by half. Stir in the clementine segments. Remove from heat and whisk in the Greek yoghurt.

Drain and mash the potatoes, add the fennel and fold in the Greek yoghurt.

Slice the chicken and serve it placed on top of the mash. This is lovely with greens or a fresh salad.

LAMB SLIDERS WITH SWEET TOMATO CHUTNEY AND CORIANDER YOGHURT

 Sliders sell more than anything on my menu and these lamb patties with sweet tomato chutney and herbed Greek yoghurt are so moreish. For a drinks party these work really well as they are both simple to make and filling.

MAKES 8 MINI SLIDERS

FOR THE SLIDERS
800g lamb leg steaks, roughly cubed,
    or minced lamb
8 mini burger buns, halved
sea salt and freshly ground black pepper

FOR THE CHUTNEY
1 onion, finely diced
5cm piece of fresh ginger, peeled and finely
    chopped
1 red chilli, finely diced
400g can chopped tomatoes
1 teaspoon yellow mustard seeds
1 teaspoon smoked paprika
½ teaspoon black mustard seeds
150g brown sugar
100ml white wine vinegar

FOR THE CORIANDER YOGHURT
170g 0% Greek yoghurt
small handful of fresh coriander leaves

If cooking on a barbecue, preheat it now.

For the chutney, place all the ingredients in a medium saucepan and bring to the boil, then reduce the heat and simmer for approximately 1 hour or until the mixture is thick and glossy. Remove from the heat and set aside to cool.

For the coriander yoghurt, blitz the yoghurt and coriander with salt and pepper in a food-processor until smooth and then chill.

If using lamb steak, mince it first by blitzing in a food-processor until coarsely chopped. Transfer the minced lamb to a large bowl and season well. Shape into 8 equal-sized patties, about 100g each.

Preheat a griddle pan over a high heat.

Barbecue or griddle the burgers for about 3 minutes on each side. For extra flavour, the buns can also be chargrilled for 30 seconds.

To serve, spread a layer of chutney on the base of each bun. Top with a burger, add a dollop of coriander yoghurt and top with the remaining bun half. Serve immediately.

VARIATION
For an added extra, melt some goats' cheese on top of the sliders.

SPICED LAMB FILLET WITH QUINOA, POMEGRANATE AND MINT SALAD

 Quinoa is the superfood grain of the moment. It's full of proteins and amino acids and is a great grain for people who are gluten intolerant. I put this salad together when I was living in Beirut. The pomegranate molasses lends the perfect acidity and sweetness. Pomegranate is also a superfood, so this salad will give you a real boost. The tahini yoghurt dressing works well as a crudité dip, too.

SERVES 4

FOR THE QUINOA SALAD
200g quinoa
seeds from 1 pomegranate
small handful of mint, torn
3 spring onions, sliced
150g radishes, sliced
½ cucumber, diced

FOR THE SALAD DRESSING
2 tablespoons pomegranate molasses
1 teaspoon ground sumac
3 tablespoons lemon juice
3 tablespoons olive oil

FOR THE YOGHURT DRESSING
1 tablespoon tahini
1 teaspoon runny honey
1 garlic clove, finely chopped
150g 2% Greek yoghurt

FOR THE LAMB
4 lamb fillets, approximately 150g each
salt and freshly ground black pepper

Prepare the quinoa according to the packet instructions and set aside to cool.

Make the salad dressing by combining all the ingredients in a small jug. Season, whisk well and set aside.

Make the yoghurt dressing by combining all the ingredients in another small jug. Season, whisk well and set aside.

Combine all the salad ingredients together in a large bowl and drizzle the salad dressing over.

Season the lamb and heat a large frying or griddle pan over a high heat. Cook the lamb for 4–5 minutes on each side – the centre of the fillets should still be pink. Cover with foil and set aside to rest for 5 minutes, then slice each fillet.

To serve, divide the salad between four plates, top with the lamb and drizzle over the yoghurt dressing.

GREEK-STYLE LAMB FLATBREADS
WITH MINT AND POMEGRANATE

 I used to buy these flatbreads from a tiny bakery on the corner of my street in Beirut. Freshly cooked to order, they were the best snack ever, straight from the oven, rolled up and devoured.

MAKES 8 TOPPED FLATBREADS

FOR THE FLATBREADS
400g strong bread flour or Italian 00 plain flour, plus extra for dusting
1 medium free-range egg, beaten
250g Classic Greek yoghurt
3 tablespoons olive oil, plus extra for oiling
sea salt

FOR THE LAMB TOPPING
1 tablespoon olive oil
1 onion, finely chopped
2 garlic cloves, finely chopped
400g minced lamb
½ teaspoon ground cinnamon
½ teaspoon ground allspice
pinch of ground cumin
pinch of ground coriander
1 tablespoon tomato purée
1 tablespoon pomegranate molasses, plus extra to drizzle (optional)
200g Classic Greek yoghurt
freshly ground black pepper

TO SERVE
3 tablespoons pine nuts
a small handful of chopped mint
100g pomegranate seeds
green herb salad

For the flatbreads, mix the flour, egg, yoghurt and olive oil together in a medium bowl. Season with salt and knead to form a smooth dough. Cover and chill in the fridge until needed.

For the lamb topping, heat the oil in a large saucepan over a medium heat, add the onion, garlic and lamb and stir until well combined. Cook for 10 minutes, stirring occasionally, until the ingredients start to turn golden and come together. Add the spices, cook for a few more minutes, then add the tomato purée and season with salt and pepper. Stir in the pomegranate molasses, then remove the pan from the heat.

Preheat the oven to 180°C/gas mark 4.

Take the flatbread dough from the fridge and turn it out onto a lightly floured surface. Roll the dough into a ball, then divide it into 8 pieces (for medium-sized flatbreads) or 24 pieces (for bite-sized flatbreads). Roll each piece into a circle, flatten it with the heel of your hand and then roll into a thin disc with a rolling pin. Place the discs onto baking trays and spread some of the lamb mixture over the top. Spread some yoghurt over the lamb and bake for 15 minutes, or until crisp and golden.

Remove from the oven and serve topped with the pine nuts, mint and pomegranate seeds. Drizzle the lamb flatbreads with the extra pomegranate molasses, if using, and serve with a green herb salad.

BAKED ORZO AND LAMB WITH
YOGHURT AND TOMATO SAUCE

 I love big one-pot suppers and this is one of my favourites as it fills the kitchen with the aromas of cinnamon, tomatoes and oregano and takes me right back to Greece in an instant. My family have lived there for 10 years now, in a 200-year-old village house. I love it there – it's worlds away from my hectic life in London. I like to bake this dish in an earthenware casserole and then just plonk it on the table with a tomato, red onion and olive salad so everyone can simply help themselves.

SERVES 4

100ml extra-virgin olive oil
750g lamb shoulder, diced into 2cm cubes
2 onions, finely chopped
1 carrot, diced
2 celery sticks, diced
4 garlic cloves, finely chopped
2 bay leaves
2 cinnamon sticks
1 teaspoon dried chilli flakes
1 teaspoon dried oregano
200ml red wine
400g can chopped tomatoes
1 litre hot vegetable stock
300g orzo pasta
340g 2% Greek yoghurt
salt and freshly ground black pepper

FOR THE TOMATO SALAD

8 ripe tomatoes, finely sliced
1 red onion, finely sliced
10 black olives, pitted

Heat the oil in a large heavy-based flameproof casserole over a medium heat, season the lamb and fry until browned, for about 10 minutes.

Add the vegetables and garlic to the casserole and cook, stirring, for a further 5 minutes. Add the bay leaves, cinnamon sticks, chilli and oregano and cook for a further minute before adding the wine. Bring the liquid to the boil and add the tomatoes and stock, bring to the boil again, then reduce the heat and simmer, uncovered, for approximately 1½ hours, until the meat is tender.

Preheat the oven to 180°C/gas mark 4.

Season the casserole to taste, then remove the bay leaves and cinnamon sticks and add the orzo. Stir well, then cook the casserole, uncovered, in the oven for 20 minutes.

Meanwhile, place the salad ingredients in a salad bowl and mix together.

Remove the casserole from the oven, spoon the yoghurt on top and roughly spread it over the surface. Increase the oven temperature to 200°C/gas mark 6, then return the casserole to the oven and bake for a final 10 minutes.

Serve the meat and pasta with the salad.

CALVES' LIVER WITH APPLE AND CALVADOS YOGHURT

When you grow up, liver always seems to be super off-putting and I am sure it's due to it often being overcooked. The truth is liver is a great source of protein, very rich in iron, so quick to cook and not too expensive. You can buy it in most supermarkets now, too.

SERVES 2

25g butter
1 apple, cored and quartered
small handful of chopped sage
50g brown sugar
50ml Calvados or brandy
170g Classic Greek yoghurt
4 slices of calves' liver
watercress, to serve

Melt the butter in a small pan and cook the apple, sage and sugar for about 8 minutes until caramelised. Pour in the Calvados or brandy. Set aside to cool. Once cooled, fold the mixture into the yoghurt.

Heat a frying pan over a medium heat and pan-fry the calves' liver to your liking. I like to keep it pink inside, so cook it for about 6 minutes on each side, depending on thickness.

Serve the liver with the apple yoghurt on the side and a little watercress.

SPICY LAMB AND CHICKPEA PASTIES WITH A MINT AND MANGO DIP

One from the Total Greek Yoghurt archives, these are spicy little parcels that are great to make and have as a picnic or packed lunch.

MAKES 8–10 PASTIES

FOR THE FILLING
50ml olive oil
1 red onion, diced
½ teaspoon chopped red chilli
2 garlic cloves, crushed
½ teaspoon ground cumin
½ teaspoon ground cinnamon
400g cooked roast lamb, diced into 1cm cubes
400g can chickpeas, rinsed and drained
handful of coriander leaves
4 tablespoons tomato purée
salt and freshly ground black pepper

FOR THE PASTRY
500g ready-made shortcrust pastry
2 medium free-range egg yolks, beaten

FOR THE TOMATO, YOGHURT AND MINT DIP
200g Classic Greek yoghurt
4 tomatoes, diced
1 tablespoon mango chutney
small bunch of mint, chopped

Place the oil in a medium pan over a medium heat. Gently fry the onion, chilli, garlic and spices for a few minutes. Add the cooked lamb and cook for 5 minutes to warm through.

Add the chickpeas and coriander and season to taste. Cook for a further 5 minutes. Remove from the heat, stir in the tomato purée and leave to cool.

Preheat the oven to 180°C/gas mark 4.

Roll out the pastry to about 5mm thick, then cut out 8–10 circles using a 5cm saucer. Brush the edges of the circles with egg yolk.

Divide the filling equally between the centre of the pastry circles, bring the edges together at the top and crimp the edges together. Place the pasties on non-stick baking trays, brush with egg yolk and bake for 20–25 minutes.

For the dip, mix the yoghurt, diced tomatoes, chutney and chopped mint together.

Serve the pasties hot or cold with the yoghurt dip.

PASTITSIO

Pastitsio is a classic Greek dish, almost like a Greek lasagne. It's incredibly comforting, and I love the way cinnamon is used with the lamb sauce – it's warming and aromatic. Usually you would top it with an egg-enriched wobbly layer of béchamel, but I have used Greek yoghurt instead – it's lower in fat and I like the freshness and tangy flavour.

SERVES 4

FOR THE SAUCE
150ml extra-virgin olive oil
1kg minced lamb
4 garlic cloves, finely diced
1 large onion, finely diced
1 teaspoon chopped fresh rosemary
2 bay leaves
1 cinnamon stick
1 teaspoon dried oregano
100ml red wine
400ml passata
1 tablespoon tomato purée
sea salt and freshly ground black pepper

FOR THE PASTA AND TOPPING
500g penne
4 medium free-range egg yolks
500g Classic Greek yoghurt
½ teaspoon freshly ground nutmeg
200g Graviera or Parmesan cheese, grated
tomato salad, to serve

Heat the olive oil in a large, heavy-based saucepan and add the lamb, garlic and onion. Season and cook for about 15 minutes, over a high heat, to brown the meat.

Add the rosemary, bay leaves, cinnamon stick, oregano, red wine and passata. Bring to the boil and simmer for about 40 minutes, season to taste, add the tomato purée, cook for a few more minutes and then remove from the heat.

Preheat the oven to 180°C/gas mark 4.

Bring a large pan of water to the boil and cook the penne according to the packet instructions. Drain the pasta and rinse it under cold running water. Mix the pasta with the sauce and pour into a 15 x 20cm baking dish.

For the topping, mix the egg yolks, yoghurt and nutmeg together, then spoon and spread over the pasta. Sprinkle with the cheese and bake for 15 minutes.

Serve the pastitsio with a tomato salad.

SWEET
PLATES,
SHAKES
&
SMOOTHIES

APPLE AND BLACKBERRY
BIRCHER MUESLI

 This is a simple and nutritious breakfast that can be varied with different fruits and berries.

FOR THE DRY MUESLI MIX (MAKES 20 SERVINGS)

1kg oats
500g flaked almonds
200g golden raisins
100g sunflower seeds
100g pumpkin seeds
2 teaspoons ground cinnamon

TO SERVE (PER PORTION)
100ml apple juice
½ green tart apple (Granny Smith is great)
100g 0% Greek yoghurt
50g blackberries

Make the dry muesli mix by combining all the dry ingredients. This mix will keep in an airtight container for several weeks.

The night before you want to eat the bircher muesli, mix 100g of the dry mixture with the apple juice and grated apple. Leave to soak overnight and then stir in the yoghurt to serve. Top with blackberries.

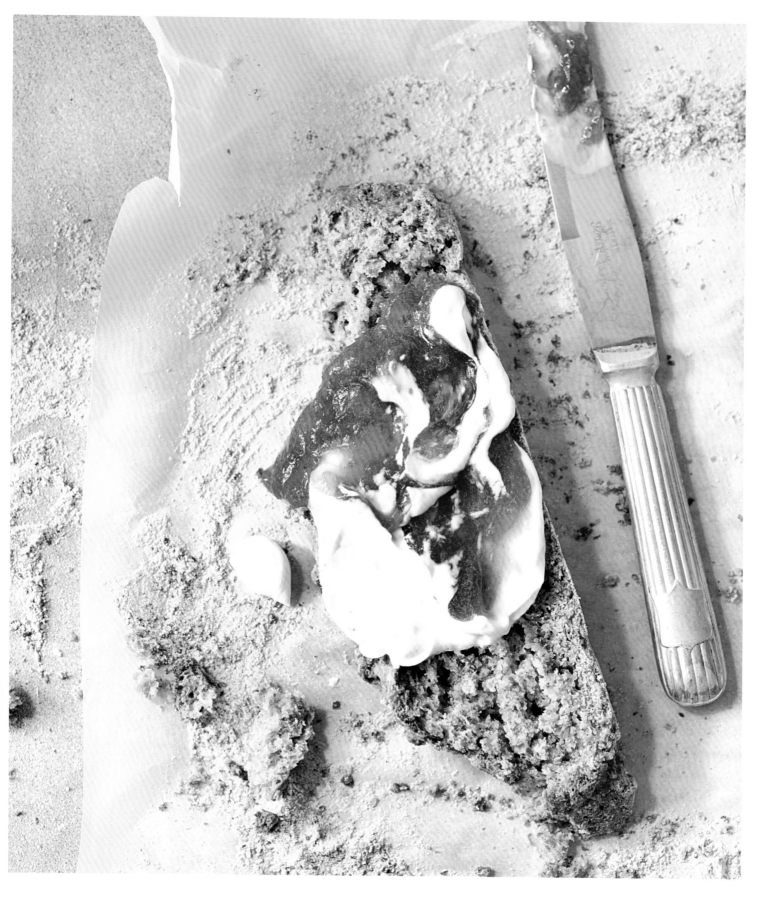

SODA BREAD WITH RHUBARB AND STRAWBERRY JAM

 This is a really easy bread to bake. If you pull out a jar of homemade jam and warm soda bread for breakfast or brunch, your friends and family will think you are amazing. In Ireland they use buttermilk for the dough, but Greek yoghurt works just as well. I serve it with yoghurt on the side too – it feels a bit like a giant cream tea.

SERVES 8

FOR THE JAM
1kg rhubarb, cut into 2cm pieces
500g strawberries, quartered
300g jam sugar
juice of 1 lemon

FOR THE BREAD
250g wholemeal flour
200g plain flour, plus extra for dusting
1 teaspoon bicarbonate of soda
1 teaspoon caster sugar
1 teaspoon salt
50g butter, melted
200ml milk (any type)
400g Classic Greek yoghurt

Place all the jam ingredients in a medium, heavy-based saucepan. Bring to the boil, then reduce the heat and simmer for approximately 1 hour, skimming the surface for scum as you go along.

To test if the jam is ready, chill a saucer in the freezer. Place a spoonful of jam on the cold saucer, then run your finger through the jam. If it ripples and feels set, then it's ready; if not, allow it to simmer for a further 15 minutes and test again.

Preheat the oven to 180°C/gas mark 4.

Put the wholemeal and plain flours, bicarbonate of soda, caster sugar and salt in a large bowl and mix until well combined.

Mix the melted butter, milk and half the yoghurt together in a jug. Make a well in the centre of the dry ingredients and gradually pour in the yoghurt mixture, then bring the dry and wet ingredients together, using your hands, until just combined. Don't overwork the mixture.

Turn the dough out onto a lightly floured surface and mould into a circle about 15cm across. Cut a deep cross in the centre, dust the top with flour and transfer to a baking tray. Bake for 30 minutes, until golden brown. Remove from the oven and leave to cool a little on a wire rack.

Serve the warm bread with the jam and a large dollop of the remaining yoghurt.

YOGHURT COATED BANANA CHIPS

 This is a super simple snack that is easy to prepare and really tasty.

SERVES 2 AS A SNACK

200g white chocolate, broken into pieces
150g icing sugar, sieved
170g Classic Greek yoghurt
200g dried banana chips

Line a baking tray with baking parchment.

Place the chocolate pieces, icing sugar and yoghurt in a heatproof bowl. Place the bowl over a pan of barely simmering water and stir until the chocolate has melted and a smooth mixture is formed.

Dip the banana chips into the mixture and place on the baking tray. Transfer to the fridge to set for about 30 minutes.

These will keep in an airtight container in the fridge for about a week.

HOT CROSS BUN AND BLUEBERRY STACKS

A fab way to use up stale hot cross buns.

SERVES 4

4 hot cross buns, halved
100ml whole milk
2 medium free-range eggs
splash of sunflower oil
2 x 170g 0% Greek yoghurt split pots with blueberry compote
1 tablespoon runny honey
50g toasted flaked almonds
200g fresh blueberries

Place the halved buns in a shallow dish. Mix the milk and eggs together in a small jug, pour over the buns and allow them to soak for a couple of minutes.

Heat the oil in a large, non-stick frying pan and gently fry the buns on each side until golden brown.

To serve, allow 2 slices per person. Top each one with yoghurt and blueberry compote, drizzle with honey and finish with almonds and fresh blueberries.

YOGHURT, BANANA AND VANILLA PANCAKES

 Pancakes are my Sunday morning staple, so I often try to think of ways to make them healthier, as well as quick, easy and tasty. The Greek yoghurt is the main binding agent here and adds richness and protein. You can replace the bananas with all sorts of fruit, too – blueberries work well, as do raspberries.

SERVES 4

170g 2% Greek yoghurt, plus extra to serve
1 large egg, beaten
½ teaspoon vanilla extract
100g self-raising flour
1 teaspoon baking powder
1 teaspoon ground cinnamon
50ml coconut or sunflower oil
2 bananas, thinly sliced
maple syrup, to serve

In a medium-sized bowl, mix the yoghurt, egg and vanilla extract together with 2 tablespoons of cold water.

Place the flour, baking powder and cinnamon in a separate, large bowl and stir to mix. Pour the yoghurt mixture into the dry ingredients and stir well to combine.

Heat about 1 teaspoon of the oil in a medium non-stick frying pan and, when hot, spoon 2 dessertspoons of the pancake mixture into the pan. Allow it to settle for a minute, then top with a few banana slices and cook for 2 minutes before flipping over with a spatula and cooking for a further 2 minutes on the other side. Transfer to a warm plate in a low oven whilst you cook the remainder. Repeat to use up the remaining batter and bananas, to make approximately 8 pancakes in total.

Serve the pancakes with an extra dollop of yoghurt and a drizzle of maple syrup.

BANANA BREAD WITH APPLE AND MAPLE SYRUP TOPPING

Using Greek yoghurt in the banana bread adds moisture and lightness, as well as replacing some of the fats.

SERVES 12

FOR THE BREAD
70g 0% Greek yoghurt
2 ripe bananas
45g caster sugar
200g self-raising flour
170g butter, plus extra for greasing
1 medium free-range egg
½ teaspoon baking powder
few drops of vanilla extract
1 teaspoon ground cinnamon

FOR THE TOPPING
100g 0% Greek yoghurt
2 tablespoons maple syrup
2 tablespoons low-sugar apple compote

Preheat the oven to 160°C/gas mark 3. Grease a 450g loaf tin and line with baking parchment.

Place all the bread ingredients in a food processor and blend until well combined.

Pour the mixture into the lined loaf tin and bake for 1 hour. You can check to see if the bread is done by inserting a skewer into the centre of the loaf. If the skewer comes out clean, the loaf is ready.

Allow the loaf to cool for at least 30 minutes in the tin and then turn out onto a wire rack.

Mix the yoghurt and maple syrup together in a bowl, spread onto the loaf and top with the apple compote. Slice to serve. The loaf will keep for a few days in an airtight container, but once you have added the topping it should be eaten at once.

BY USING TOTAL GREEK YOGHURT, YOU'VE ADDED NEARLY 18G PROTEIN TO YOUR CAKE

PINK PEPPERCORN AND STRAWBERRY SHORTCAKES

 I've always been told that the flavours of black pepper and strawberry go well together and they do. I prefer to use pink peppercorns, as quite apart from the obvious feminine colour, they are more aromatic and slightly gentler. Shortcakes are a USA invention – like a scone and sponge rolled into one, and rather lovely.

MAKES 6 SHORTCAKES

400g strawberries, sliced
50g icing sugar, sifted, plus extra for dusting
1 teaspoon dried pink peppercorns, crushed
300g Classic Greek yoghurt

FOR THE SHORTCAKES

350g self-raising flour, plus extra for dusting
100g chilled unsalted butter, cubed
75g caster sugar
pinch of salt
100ml whole milk, warmed
1 medium free-range egg, plus a little extra beaten egg for glazing

Place the strawberries, icing sugar and peppercorns in a bowl. Mix well and leave to macerate.

Preheat the oven to 220°C/gas mark 7 and lightly flour a baking sheet.

Put the flour, butter, sugar and salt in the bowl of a food processor, then pulse until the mixture resembles fine breadcrumbs.

In a small jug, beat the milk and egg together, then pour it into the mixture and blitz to form an uneven dough. Tip the dough out onto a floured surface and bring it together with your hands. Shape the dough into a smooth disc and roll it out to a thickness of 2cm. Using a 4cm plain round cutter, stamp out 6 circles.

Transfer the rounds to the floured baking sheet and brush with the beaten egg, to glaze. Bake for 10–12 minutes until risen and golden. Cool on a wire rack then cut in half.

To serve, spoon some yoghurt onto the bottom half of each shortcake biscuit, spoon over some of the strawberries and then top with the other half of the shortcake. Dust with sieved icing sugar and serve immediately.

BY USING TOTAL GREEK YOGHURT INSTEAD OF CLOTTED CREAM FOR THESE SHORTCAKES, YOU'VE REDUCED THE FAT INTAKE OF THIS DISH BY 92%

SOUR CHERRY AND YOGHURT CAKE

 This rich, dense cake is lifted by the lovely, tangy note of sour cherries. If you like, you can also try making it with different fruits, such as apricots or blackberries, but to me, this combination is best. It's perfect served with a big dollop of Classic Greek yoghurt and a strong mid-morning coffee.

SERVES 12

200g unsalted butter, at room temperature, plus
    extra for greasing
200g caster sugar
4 medium free-range eggs
100g Classic Greek yoghurt, plus extra to serve
200g self-raising flour
1 teaspoon baking powder
150g frozen sour cherries, defrosted and drained

Preheat the oven to 180°C/gas mark 4. Grease a 450g loaf tin.

In a bowl, beat the butter and sugar together until light and fluffy. In a separate bowl, beat the eggs together and then gradually add a spoonful at a time to the butter mixture, whisking well in between. If the mixture starts to curdle, add a little of the flour to bind it.

When all the eggs have been added, stir through the Greek yoghurt and fold in the flour and baking powder. Pour into the greased loaf tin and scatter the cherries on top. Bake for 25–30 minutes or until a skewer inserted into the centre comes out clean.

Remove the cake from the tin and cool on a wire rack. Slice and serve with an extra dollop of yoghurt. This cake will keep for up to 3 days in an airtight container.

THIS RECIPE REPLACES 100G OF THE BUTTER YOU'D NORMALLY FIND IN THIS SORT OF CAKE WITH TOTAL GREEK YOGHURT, WHICH SHAVES OFF JUST OVER 640 CALORIES

TOTAL +2

With the addition of just a couple of ingredients, you can turn your Greek yoghurt into a delicious and healthy dessert or tempting sweet snack. For some savoury +2 options, see page 59.

POMEGRANATE AND PISTACHIO

SERVES 1

1 tablespoon pomegranate seeds
½ tablespoon pistachios
170g Classic Greek yoghurt

Scatter the pomegranate seeds and pistachios over
the yoghurt.

ROSE PETAL JAM AND FIG

SERVES 1

½ tablespoon rose petal jam (available in Middle-
    Eastern stores and Mediterranean delis)
170g Classic Greek yoghurt
1 fresh fig, quartered

Mix the jam into the yoghurt and serve with the fig.

MANGO AND CHILLI

SERVES 1

½ mango, peeled and diced
1 teaspoon finely diced red chilli, deseeded
170g Classic Greek yoghurt

Mix the mango and chilli together. Set aside for 10
minutes, then stir through the yoghurt.

RASPBERRY AND VANILLA

SERVES 1

½ vanilla pod, seeds only
2 tablespoons raspberries
170g Classic Greek yoghurt

Mix the vanilla seeds and raspberries through the
yoghurt.

PEANUT BUTTER AND CHOCOLATE

SERVES 1

1½ tablespoons smooth peanut butter
170g Classic Greek yoghurt
1 tablespoon grated good-quality dark chocolate,
    minimum 70% cocoa solids

Stir the peanut butter through the yoghurt until
thoroughly combined and then top with the dark
chocolate.

WHITE PEACH AND ALMOND

SERVES 1

1 tablespoon roughly chopped blanched almonds,
    toasted
170g Classic Greek yoghurt
1 white peach, peeled, halved, stoned and sliced

Sprinkle the almonds over the yoghurt and serve
with the peach.

RED VELVET CUPCAKES WITH YOGHURT FROSTING

 Red velvet cupcakes are one of the bestsellers at my restaurant, Pont St – everyone loves them. Here, the yoghurt makes a lovely, light frosting that is healthier than the traditional, calorie-intense butter and cream cheese topping.

MAKES 12 CUPCAKES

120g unsalted butter, at room temperature
300g caster sugar
2 large eggs
240g 0% Greek yoghurt
2 tablespoons red food colouring
1 teaspoon vanilla extract
1 teaspoon white wine vinegar
1 teaspoon baking powder
250g self-raising flour
20g cocoa powder

FOR THE ICING

125g icing sugar
250g cream cheese
400g Classic Greek yoghurt
1 teaspoon vanilla extract

Preheat the oven to 180°C/gas mark 4. Line a 12-hole muffin tray with cupcake cases.

In a bowl, cream the butter and sugar together, then add the eggs, one at a time, whisking thoroughly between each addition.

In a separate bowl, mix the yoghurt and red colouring together, then add the vanilla extract, vinegar and baking powder and stir to combine. Pour this into the wet mixture, stir to combine and fold in the sifted flour and cocoa powder.

Divide the cake mix between the cupcake cases and bake for 20 minutes until risen. Transfer to a wire rack to cool.

To make the icing, sieve the icing sugar into a medium bowl, add the cream cheese and beat until smooth, then mix in the yoghurt and vanilla extract.

When the cakes are completely cold, use a spatula or butter knife to spread the icing over each one. If you prefer to use a piping bag, spoon the icing into a piping bag fitted with a star nozzle. Pipe the icing, using a spiralling motion, onto the cupcakes in large swirls. These will keep in the fridge in an airtight container for about 3 days.

CARROT AND YOGHURT CAKE

This lightly spiced carrot cake is made even more moist with the Greek yoghurt in the batter and the topping. Lightly spiced and with a slightly virtuous feeling.

SERVES 10

butter, for greasing
150g carrot, grated
200g Classic Greek yoghurt
200ml orange juice
75g muscovado sugar
75g sultanas
75g sunflower seeds
50ml sunflower oil
3 medium free-range eggs, beaten
½ teaspoon vanilla extract
300g wholemeal flour
100g self-raising flour
1½ teaspoons bicarbonate of soda
2 teaspoons ground cinnamon
1 teaspoon mixed spice

FOR THE ICING

200g cream cheese
100g 0% Greek yoghurt
50g icing sugar, sifted
½ tablespoon vanilla extract

Preheat the oven to 160°C/gas mark 3. Lightly grease a 30 x 20cm cake tin.

Mix the carrot, yoghurt, orange juice, sugar, sultanas, sunflower seeds, oil, eggs, and vanilla in a large mixing bowl.

In a separate large bowl, thoroughly mix the flours, bicarbonate of soda, cinnamon and mixed spice. Fold the dry ingredients gradually into the carrot mixture until blended.

Spoon the mixture into the prepared cake tin, and bake for 1 hour. Insert a skewer into the middle of the cake to check that it is cooked through. If it comes out clean, the cake is ready.

Remove from the oven and turn out onto a wire rack. Allow to cool for 2 hours or until completely cold.

Meanwhile, for the frosting, whisk all the ingredients together and then spread on top of the cake when cooled.

Cut the cake into squares. This will keep in an airtight container for up to 5 days.

BAKED PUMPKIN AND GINGER TART

I made my first Thanksgiving dinner at Belgraves Hotel last year – what an eye opener, and what a great menu! Pumpkin all ways, whipped and topped with marshmallows, in pies and cupcakes – it was everywhere! This is a classic pumpkin pie that would be great to prepare for Thanksgiving or Halloween.

SERVES 8

FOR THE PASTRY
200g plain flour, plus extra for dusting
pinch of salt
100g unsalted butter, at room temperature

FOR THE FILLING
500g pumpkin, peeled, seeds removed and cut into large chunks
2 medium free-range eggs
20g stem ginger in syrup, drained and diced
100g caster sugar
¼ teaspoon ground cloves
¼ teaspoon ground cinnamon
¼ teaspoon freshly grated nutmeg
Classic Greek yoghurt and icing sugar, to serve

Preheat the oven to 200°C/gas mark 6.

To make the pastry, place all the ingredients in a food processor and whizz to form a dough – don't overwork it. Wrap the dough in clingfilm and chill in the fridge for 30 minutes.

On a lightly floured work surface, roll the dough out into a circle approximately ½cm thick. Line a 30cm fluted loose-based tart tin with the pastry and then press down carefully. Top with baking parchment and fill the pastry case with baking beans. Bake blind for 30 minutes until the edges are starting to brown. Remove the beans and baking parchment, trim the edges and then return to the oven to cook the base of the pastry for a further 10 minutes.

Meanwhile, place the pumpkin chunks in a steamer and steam for 15–20 minutes, or until tender. Remove from the steamer and allow to cool.

Place the pumpkin into a food processor and blend to a purée. Then add the eggs, ginger, sugar, cloves, cinnamon and nutmeg and whizz to make the filling.

Pour the pumpkin mixture into the pastry case and bake for 40–45 minutes, or until the filling has set. Remove from the oven and cool for at least 2 hours.

To serve, cut into portions, spoon over some Greek yoghurt and dust with icing sugar.

PLUM CINNAMON CRUMBLE TART

 The yoghurt topping on these deep purple plums and spiced crumble is autumn in a slice. I am a great believer in seasonal shopping and there is so much you can make during the autumn season – jams, chutneys, tarts – it's a time to look forward to as a chef and marks the lead-up to Christmas.

SERVES 16

FOR THE PASTRY
200g plain flour, plus extra for dusting
pinch of salt
100g unsalted butter, at room temperature

FOR THE CRUMBLE
150g unsalted butter
300g plain flour
100g demerara sugar
½ teaspoon mixed spice
1 teaspoon ground cinnamon

FOR THE FILLING
350g Classic Greek yoghurt, plus extra to serve
2 egg yolks
500g deep purple plums, halved and stoned

Preheat the oven to 200°C/gas mark 6.

To make the pastry, place all the ingredients in a food processor and whizz to form a dough – don't overwork it. Wrap the dough in clingfilm and chill in the fridge for 30 minutes.

On a lightly floured work surface, roll the dough out into a circle approximately ½cm thick. Line a 30cm fluted loose-based tart tin with the pastry and then press down carefully. Top with baking parchment and fill the pastry case with baking beans. Bake blind for 30 minutes until the edges are starting to brown. Remove the beans and baking parchment, trim the edges and then return to the oven to cook the base of the pastry for a further 10 minutes.

Meanwhile, make the crumble. Place the butter, flour, sugar and spices in a medium bowl. Rub the butter in until the mixture resembles rough breadcrumbs.

For the filling, mix the yoghurt and egg yolks together in a jug and pour into the base.

Arrange the plum halves, cut-side up, on top. Sprinkle the crumble topping over and bake for 20 minutes or until the topping is golden brown.

Remove from the oven and serve at room temperature with extra Greek yoghurt on the side.

CRANBERRY OATMEAL BARS

These yummy oat bars are ideal healthy lunchbox fillers for all the family. Full of fibre, they'll help ward off the hunger pains all day!

MAKES 24 BARS

100g plain white flour
100g oats
100g macadamia nuts, roughly chopped
50g brown sugar
¼ teaspoon salt
¼ teaspoon bicarbonate of soda
½ teaspoon ground cinnamon
50g unsalted butter, melted
50ml sunflower oil
50ml apple juice

FOR THE FILLING

100g dried cranberries
75g 0% Greek yoghurt
50g caster sugar
30g plain white flour
1 large egg white, lightly beaten

Preheat the oven to 160°C/gas mark 3. Line a 24 x 18cm baking tin with baking parchment or use a non-stick tin.

In a medium bowl mix together the flour, oats, nuts, sugar, salt, bicarbonate of soda, and cinnamon.

In a separate bowl, mix the butter, oil and apple juice together and fold into the flour and oat mix to form a moist and crumbly mix.

Press three-quarters of the oat mixture into the bottom of the prepared tin and set the remaining mixture to one side.

Now make the filling. In a separate bowl, mix together the cranberries, Greek yoghurt, sugar, flour and egg white. Spread the yoghurt mixture evenly over the prepared base and then sprinkle the remaining oat mixture on top.

Bake for 40 minutes or until the edges are golden. Remove from the oven and score the top with a knife to mark out the bars. Allow to cool in the tin for 10 minutes, then remove from the tin and cut into bars. Transfer the bars to a wire rack and leave to cool completely. They will keep in an airtight container for about 1 week.

CHOCOLATE AND TIA MARIA
FRIDGE CAKE

Rich, creamy, crunchy, with a little boozy boost, this recipe requires no cooking so is great to throw together and will be a big hit. This is a recipe from the Total Greek Yoghurt archive that replaces the usual cream with yoghurt. I also serve some extra yoghurt on the side as it cuts through the richness.

SERVES 10

500g good-quality dark chocolate, minimum
    70% cocoa solids, broken into pieces
250ml double cream
250g 2% Greek yoghurt, plus extra to serve
75ml strong black coffee
75ml Tia Maria
5 tablespoons glucose syrup
200g shortbread biscuits, roughly crushed
100g glacé cherries, left whole
mint leaves, to decorate (optional)

Place the chocolate in a large heatproof bowl over a pan of barely simmering water. Stir occasionally until melted.

In a separate bowl, lightly whip the double cream, then fold in the yoghurt. Set aside.

Mix the coffee and Tia Maria together in a small pan and warm through. Add the glucose syrup and stir to incorporate.

When the chocolate has melted, pour in the coffee mix, and then fold in the broken biscuits and cherries. Now start to fold the cream and yoghurt into the chocolate mix until well combined. Pour the mixture into a 25cm round springform cake tin, smooth the surface and refrigerate for 12 hours.

To serve, turn the cake out onto a board and cut into 10 slices. Decorate each slice with a sprig of mint (if using) and serve with a dollop of yoghurt.

GREEN TEA FROZEN ÉCLAIRS

 Green tea, baby! The ultimate health ingredient right now. Matcha green tea powder is an amazing ingredient. I drink it as much as possible, but cooking with it is brilliant too. Chocolates, crème brûlées, ice creams, custards – all work brilliantly with green tea. Frozen yoghurt is excellent too, and sandwiched up with choux buns the flavour is gorgeous. You'll need an ice-cream maker for this recipe.

MAKES 12

FOR THE CHOUX PASTRY
oil, for greasing
50g unsalted butter
75g plain flour, plus extra for dusting
2 medium free-range eggs, beaten

FOR THE FROZEN YOGHURT
500g 2% Greek yoghurt
150g agave syrup
50g good-quality matcha green tea powder, plus
　　extra for dusting and decorating

Preheat the oven to 200°C/gas mark 6. Lightly oil and flour a baking sheet.

Pour 150ml cold water into a medium saucepan, add the butter and bring to the boil. Reduce the heat to medium, then, stirring vigorously and continuously, tip in the flour all at once. Continue stirring until a soft paste forms and the oil from the butter starts to come to the surface. Remove the saucepan from the heat, then gradually beat in the eggs until the mixture is smooth and glossy and has a dropping consistency. Leave to cool.

Spoon the paste into a large piping bag fitted with a 2cm plain nozzle and pipe twelve blobs onto the prepared baking sheet, leaving a space between each for the éclairs to double in size during baking. Bake for 30 minutes or until cooked through, golden and crispy.

Remove the éclairs from the oven, pierce the bottoms with a skewer to release the steam and leave on a wire rack until cold.

In a medium bowl, mix the yoghurt and agave syrup together and then sift the tea powder in and mix well. Pour into an ice-cream maker and churn until thick and creamy. Spoon into a lidded plastic container and store in the freezer for at least 1 hour.

When the éclairs are cooled and the frozen yoghurt is ready, cut the éclairs in half lengthways and then spoon or pipe in the yoghurt. Place the top back on and return to the freezer. When ready to eat, sift over a little green tea powder and serve immediately.

CHOCOLATE AND PEANUT BUTTER TARTS

Peanut butter and chocolate is a craving-inducing match. Most tarts are very rich, though, and full of double cream and cream cheese. Here the yoghurt replaces some of that, and the agave replaces the sugar. It tastes great and, when tested on my usual guinea pigs (aka friends and family), it was proclaimed to be the best dessert ever by one of them.

MAKES 4 TARTS

300g chocolate cream sandwich biscuits, roughly broken
100g unsalted butter, melted
175g smooth peanut butter
175g cream cheese
2 tablespoons icing sugar
150g Classic Greek yoghurt
1 teaspoon vanilla extract
200g good-quality dark chocolate, minimum 70% cocoa solids, grated

Blitz the biscuits in a food processor to form fine crumbs, then add the melted butter and mix well. Divide the mixture evenly between four 8cm tartlet tins. Press the mixture into the tins and up the sides, using the back of a metal spoon. Then chill in the fridge for 1 hour.

Meanwhile, spoon the peanut butter into a bowl and mix well, then add the cream cheese and mix again until smooth. Sieve in the icing sugar and then add the yoghurt and vanilla extract and mix well. Either pipe this mix into the tart cases with a plain nozzle or spoon it in. Finish off with the grated dark chocolate. These can be made up to one day in advance.

STICKY GINGERBREAD AND PECAN PUDDING WITH GINGER AND RUM YOGHURT

You need a good pudding recipe every now and again and this is the kind of pudding I would serve on Christmas day, a worthy replacement for the rich traditional Christmas offering. The rum and ginger yoghurt is great, but you can use brandy or Gran Marnier instead if you prefer.

SERVES 4

100ml ginger wine
100ml rum
50g soft brown sugar
75g self-raising flour, plus extra for dusting
¼ teaspoon baking powder
½ teaspoon bicarbonate of soda
1 heaped teaspoon ground ginger
¼ teaspoon ground cinnamon
¼ teaspoon ground cloves
1 large egg
40g unsalted butter, at room temperature, plus
    extra for greasing
50g molasses sugar
50g stem ginger in syrup, drained and chopped
75g Bramley apple, peeled and chopped
75g pecans, chopped
250g Classic Greek yoghurt

Preheat the oven to 180°C/gas mark 4. Grease 4 x 175ml pudding basins with butter and dust them with flour. Place the basins on a baking tray.

Place the ginger wine, rum and soft brown sugar in a small pan, bring to a boil and simmer until it forms a syrup. Leave to cool.

In a mixing bowl, sift the flour, baking powder, bicarbonate of soda and spices, then add the egg, butter and molasses sugar.

Using a hand-held electric mixer, whisk everything together, gradually adding 75ml warm water to make a smooth mixture. Fold in the stem ginger, apple and pecans.

Divide the mixture equally between the buttered pudding basins and cook in the centre of the oven for 30–35 minutes, until they feel firm and springy to the touch.

Gently ease the puddings from their basins by running a blunt knife around the edge of each pudding, placing a plate on top of the basin and then inverting. Mix the rum and ginger wine syrup with the yoghurt and pour over the hot puddings to serve.

YOGHURT CRÈME BRÛLÉE WITH CARDAMOM CARAMEL TOPPING

 Indian desserts are often creamy, with delicate spices running through. Cardamom and saffron work particularly well and this crème brûlée was inspired by that. I have made a base with the condensed milk, yoghurt and eggs, then topped with a spicy caramel crunch topping. Crème brûlées are a great base for experimenting; I flavour them with rosewater, lavender, white chocolate, orange oil... the list is endless and when you get the hang of making them, they are an easy and very popular dessert to pull off.

SERVES 4

340g Classic Greek yoghurt
50ml condensed milk
4 medium free-range egg yolks
1 teaspoon vanilla extract

FOR THE CARAMEL

200g caster sugar
1 teaspoon black cardamom seeds

Preheat the oven to 160°C/gas mark 3.

Mix the yoghurt, condensed milk, egg yolks and vanilla together. Then pour into four 175ml ramekins. Place the ramekins in a roasting tin and half fill the tin with hot water so that it comes half way up the outside of the ramekins. Cook for 20 minutes or until just set.

Remove the ramekins from the tin, cool to room temperature and then chill in the fridge.

Once the custards are set, make the caramel. Place the sugar and cardamom seeds with 100ml cold water in a small pan and bring to the boil, being careful not to let the sugar go up the sides and not to stir, or it will crystallise. Once it starts to turn golden, watch it carefully, as it burns very quickly. When it is a medium golden colour, remove from the heat and carefully pour one-quarter over each custard.

Set aside for the caramel to cool and keep in the fridge until ready to serve.

HONEY, CINNAMON AND YOGHURT CHEESECAKE

 At our house in Crete we have an original wood-burning oven just inside the entrance to the courtyard. It's hundreds of years old and was once the main oven of the village where everyone would bake their bread, but it still works and I love to experiment with it. One summer, I made this cheesecake with a few ingredients I had to hand and I loved the flavours so much that I've made it again and again, though often in a conventional oven, which I have to admit is more predictable.

SERVES 12

300g digestive biscuits
100g unsalted butter, melted
pinch of salt

FOR THE FILLING

500g cream cheese
50g golden caster sugar
1 tablespoon cornflour
3 medium free-range eggs, beaten
200g Classic Greek yoghurt
seeds from 1 vanilla pod
150g full-flavoured runny honey
1 teaspoon ground cinnamon
200g sultanas, soaked in boiling water and drained

FOR THE TOPPING

170g Classic Greek yoghurt
1 teaspoon vanilla extract

Preheat the oven to 160°C/gas mark 3.

In a blender or large bowl, finely crush the digestive biscuits and mix thoroughly with the melted butter and a pinch of salt. Transfer the biscuit mix to a 30cm round springform cake tin and pack down carefully to cover the base. Place in the fridge to set for approximately 20 minutes.

In a large bowl, beat together the cream cheese, sugar and cornflour. Add the eggs, yoghurt and vanilla seeds, and then incorporate the honey, cinnamon and drained sultanas, stirring well to combine.

Tip the cheese mixture into the cake tin and spread to cover the biscuit base. Wrap the underside of the cake tin with foil and then place in the middle of a large, deep roasting tray. Pour hot water into the tray until it reaches half way up the sides of the cake tin, then carefully place in the oven and cook for approximately 30 minutes.

For the topping, mix the yoghurt and vanilla together in a small bowl with 50ml cold water. Remove the cheesecake from the oven and thinly spread the yoghurt topping over the surface.

Increase the oven temperature to 180°C/gas mark 4. Return the cheesecake to the oven for a further 15 minutes. When the cake is just set, take it out and set aside to cool completely. Chill the cheesecake in the fridge overnight before slicing and serving.

ORANGE BLOSSOM PANNA COTTA WITH POACHED FIGS

 I lived in Beirut for a year as a restaurant consultant and I think I fell in love with the city within the first 24 hours – especially with the flavours of Lebanese cooking. To me, adding flower water to food is incredibly romantic and I love the delicate aromatic note that orange blossom adds to this delicious set cream. The figs are so visually stunning that if you don't have time to make the panna cotta, you could simply serve them on their own with a scoop of Greek yoghurt.

SERVES 4

FOR THE PANNA COTTA
4 sheets of leaf gelatine
200ml whole milk
1 teaspoon orange blossom water
2 tablespoons runny honey
250g 0% Greek yoghurt

FOR THE POACHED FIGS
100g caster sugar
400g fresh baby figs
chopped pistachios, to decorate (optional)

Place the gelatine in a small bowl and cover with cold water, then set aside.

Place the milk in a small saucepan with the orange blossom water and honey and gently bring to the boil, then take off the heat. Squeeze out any excess water from the gelatine, then stir into the hot milk. Add the yoghurt to the pan and stir again to combine. Transfer this mixture into a jug and divide between 4 x 175ml pudding moulds. Place in the fridge and chill for 2 hours.

Meanwhile, for the poached figs, place the sugar and 100ml cold water in a saucepan and bring to the boil. Simmer for about 5–8 minutes, then add the figs and continue cooking for a few minutes until they are just about to burst, but still intact. Lift out the figs with a slotted spoon, then set aside. Bring the remaining liquid to a boil and simmer to reduce it to a syrup.

When the figs are cooled, turn the panna cotta out of their moulds onto individual dessert plates and serve with the figs, a drizzle of syrup and a sprinkling of pistachios, if using.

PASSION FRUIT AND COCONUT MERINGUE MESS

 Inspired by Eton mess, but with much more flavour. Making your own curd is a really good skill to learn, as you can experiment with flavours – just stick to an acidic fruit. This passion fruit curd goes with everything from pancakes to pavlovas and keeps for a week in the fridge. The crushed meringues add texture, the yoghurt replaces the traditional whipped cream and the sharpness of the passion fruit cuts through it all to create a truly decadent dessert.

SERVES 4

FOR THE PASSION FRUIT CURD
8 passion fruit
zest and juice of 1 lime
100g caster sugar
2 medium free-range eggs, plus 2 yolks
25g unsalted butter

FOR THE COCONUT CREAM
50ml coconut milk
1 tablespoon Malibu
150g 2% Greek yoghurt
4 shop-bought meringues
50g coconut shavings, lightly toasted in the oven

To make the passion fruit curd, halve the passion fruit and scoop the flesh and seeds into a medium saucepan, then add the lime zest and juice. Add the sugar, eggs and egg yolks and whisk until well combined, then put the saucepan over a medium heat, and stir slowly for 15 minutes until the egg mixture thickens.

Add the butter and stir quickly until it melts and the ingredients are well combined. Remove from the heat and leave to cool to room temperature, then cover with clingfilm and chill in the fridge for 1 hour.

For the coconut cream, mix the coconut milk, Malibu and yoghurt together in a large bowl.

When you are ready to serve, crush the meringues into large pieces, then fold them into the coconut yoghurt mix. Then gently fold in the passion fruit curd. Do not overmix, as you want to create a ripple effect. Spoon into individual bowls and serve sprinkled with the toasted coconut shavings.

LEMON AND BLUEBERRY TRIFLE

 This is a spring and summer trifle. It's great for Easter and is beautifully fresh with the fruit, lemons and yoghurt. We have our own lemons in Greece and they make the most amazing lemon curd, but organic unwaxed lemons are great too. My grandmother made the best trifle ever, but I think she would approve of this one.

SERVES 8

1 vanilla Swiss roll, cut into 2cm slices
50ml Limoncello (optional)

FOR THE LEMON CUSTARD

3 medium free-range egg yolks
150g caster sugar
1 tablespoon cornflour
seeds from 1 vanilla pod
300ml whole milk
zest and juice of 1 lemon
100g Classic Greek yoghurt

FOR THE BLUEBERRY COMPOTE

400g blueberries, plus extra to serve
100g caster sugar

FOR THE TOPPING

150ml double cream
150g Classic Greek yoghurt

Begin with the custard. Whisk the egg yolks, sugar, cornflour and vanilla seeds together in a heatproof bowl until combined. Pour the milk into a non-stick saucepan and bring to the boil, then pour into the egg yolk mixture, stirring continuously so that the eggs don't cook. Pour the custard mixture back into the saucepan, add the lemon zest and juice and heat very gently, stirring continuously, until thickened, then take off the heat and mix in the yoghurt. Set aside to cool.

To make the compote, place the blueberries and sugar in a small pan and bring to the boil. Simmer for 5 minutes and then take off the heat and set aside to cool at room temperature.

Lay the slices of Swiss roll carefully into the bottom of a glass serving bowl, so you can see the spirals. Drizzle the Limoncello over, if using. Spoon over the blueberry mix and top with the custard.

Finally, whisk the cream to soft peaks, add the yoghurt and mix well, then spoon over the top of the trifle. Chill in the fridge for 30 minutes then serve, topped with blueberries.

LOLLIES

 I loved creating these little pops! Frozen yoghurt has become really fashionable – I first tried it in LA, and there were queues around the block. You can make all sorts of flavours and it's healthier than shop-bought lollies and ice creams. There are so many alternatives to sugars and using honey, fruit purée, etc. makes them healthier for children and adults. These are best served next day, but will keep in the freezer for about 1 week.

AVOCADO AND AGAVE

MAKES 6–8

340g Classic Greek yoghurt
2 avocados
1 teaspoon lime juice
200g agave nectar

Place all the ingredients in a blender and blitz until smooth. Pour the mixture into 6–8 lolly moulds, freeze for 1 hour, then insert the sticks and freeze overnight. Serve the next day.

BANANA AND HONEY

MAKES 6–8

340g Classic Greek yoghurt
2 bananas
150g runny honey

Place all the ingredients in a blender and blitz until smooth. Pour the mixture into 6–8 lolly moulds, freeze for 1 hour, then insert the sticks and freeze overnight. Serve the next day.

ROSEWATER AND PISTACHIO

MAKES 6–8

1 tablespoon rosewater
100g icing sugar
340g Classic Greek yoghurt
100g chopped pistachios

Mix the rosewater, sugar and yoghurt together. Pour into 6-8 moulds. Freeze for about 1 hour, then sprinkle the bases with the chopped pistachios, insert the sticks and freeze overnight. Serve the next day.

PEACH AND HONEY

MAKES 6–8

340g Classic Greek yoghurt
2 peaches, peeled and finely diced
150g honey
1 teaspoon vanilla extract

Mix all the ingredients together. Pour the mixture into 6–8 lolly moulds, freeze for 1 hour, then insert the sticks and freeze overnight. Serve the next day.

RASPBERRY AND BLUEBERRY LAYERS

MAKES 6–8

100g icing sugar
340g Classic Greek yoghurt
50ml blueberry purée
50ml raspberry purée

Mix the icing sugar and yoghurt together. Then divide the mixture into two, add the raspberry purée to one half and the blueberry purée to the other half. Pour the blueberry mixture to half way up 6–8 moulds, then freeze for 1 hour. Insert the sticks and top up the moulds with the raspberry mixture. Freeze overnight and serve the following day.

HONEYCOMB SEMIFREDDO
WITH HOT BRANDY BANANAS

 Semifreddos of frozen parfaits are the closest you can get to making ice cream without an ice-cream maker. The '*zabaglione*' of eggs and sugar stop the cream from crystallising and it sets beautifully. A chilled slice of this with the hot brandy bananas is really good.

SERVES 4

FOR THE SEMIFREDDO
90g runny honey
4 medium free-range egg yolks, whisked
150ml double cream
150g Classic Greek yoghurt
150g honeycomb, broken up into small pieces

FOR THE BANANAS
3 bananas
25g unsalted butter
2 tablespoons brandy

Line a 450g loaf tin with clingfilm.

For the semifreddo, warm the honey slightly in a small pan and slowly pour into the eggs, whisking at the same time, until the mix is light and fluffy.

Whip the cream in a large bowl until it forms soft peaks. Fold the yoghurt into the cream and then carefully fold in the egg mixture. Finally, fold in the honeycomb and pour into the lined loaf tin. Place in the freezer overnight until frozen.

When you are ready to eat, slice the bananas. Heat up a frying pan. Add the butter, then the brandy and cook the bananas for 5 minutes.

Remove the semifreddo from the freezer and turn it out of the loaf tin. Peel off the clingfilm, then remove and slice the semifreddo and place on plates. Spoon the hot bananas over the semifreddo and serve.

APRICOT AND PISTACHIO YOG-POPS

Another idea for yoghurt pops, this one came from the Total Greek Yoghurt archives and gets a lovely crunch from the pistachios.

MAKES 6

250g Classic Greek yoghurt
250ml double cream
50g pistachios, chopped
4 tablespoons apricot jam

In a medium bowl, whisk together the Greek yoghurt and cream until thick and creamy. Fold in the pistachios and apricot jam.

Pour the mixture into 6 lolly moulds, freeze for 1 hour, then insert the sticks and freeze for a minimum of 2 hours.

COCONUT, LIME AND BANANA CRUSH

 Well we had to have one cocktail in here! This really is like an alcoholic smoothie. It goes down like a dream and floods you with memories of summer holidays, sun cream and beaches.

SERVES 6

100g Classic Greek yoghurt
100ml Malibu
100ml pineapple juice
1 banana
100ml coconut milk
zest of 1 lime
200g crushed ice

Place all the ingredients in a food processor or blender. Whizz together and divide between 6 glasses to serve.

MANGO LASSI

Mango lassis are soothing and perfect when eating spicy foods. They are also great drinks for anytime. I add salt as it balances the lassi, stopping it from being too sweet and giving it a more isotonic vibe. Good for a post work-out boost.

SERVES 2

1 ripe mango, peeled and stoned
170g 0% Greek yoghurt
100ml sparkling water
juice of 1 lime
pinch of salt
ice cubes, to serve

Place all the ingredients in a food processor or blender. Whizz together until smooth.

Place a few ice cubes in 2 glasses and pour in the lassi.

VANILLA, DATE AND PEAR SMOOTHIE

The dates that you find in the Middle East and Greece are almost like toffees and are eaten instead of sweets. This smoothie uses the dates for sweetness and then aromatic vanilla, crisp pear and smooth, creamy yoghurt.

SERVES 2

250g Classic Greek yoghurt
150ml pear juice
50g dates, stoned
handful of ice
1 vanilla pod, seeds only

Blitz all the ingredients together in a food processor or blender and pour into 2 glasses.

RASPBERRY POWER SMOOTHIE

Everyone needs a power smoothie in their recipe book and this is mine – soothing protein-packed almond milk, creamy yoghurt and sweet raspberries.

SERVES 1

150g 0% Greek yoghurt
200g raspberries
2 tablespoons oats
1 teaspoon runny honey
1 tablespoon almond butter
100ml skimmed milk
handful of ice

Place all the ingredients in a blender or food processor and whizz until smooth. Add enough cold water to reach the desired consistency.

Serve straightaway.

BY USING TOTAL GREEK YOGHURT INSTEAD OF SKIMMED MILK, YOU'VE JUST ADDED 12G OF PROTEIN TO YOUR SMOOTHIE!